DEWDROPS

A Daily Devotional

Morning Meditations to Cultivate
Faith, Love, and Service

Jessica L. Morris

Aperture Press

ISBN: 978-0-9910962-8-2
Library of Congress Control Number: 2014952857

First edition, October 2014

Book designed by Stephen Wagner.
Cover photo courtesy of Sandralise/Bigstock.com.

For all those who have helped me to find my way, and for all those who continue to help me find my way—this book of daily meditations is my way of honoring you and your service to your fellow man. Thank you for your time, energy, acceptance, and love, without which I would have remained lost.

Foreword

Being born the youngest of four children to an active alcoholic and an adult child of an alcoholic was my physical beginning. Comprehending only the type of behavior displayed by my dysfunctional family was my mental and emotional beginning. Learning about God and Jesus from my father, a Methodist minister who was also an abusive alcoholic, was my spiritual beginning.

It was a rough start. The disease of addiction flowed through my blood, I was constantly trying to be noticed by anyone who would pay attention to me, and my ideas about God consisted mostly of how much He must have hated me. Before I was old enough for school, I was using food as a sedative without knowing it. And, not long after that, I discovered that the warmth of a swift drink of alcohol—any kind—would calm my nerves and help me to do anything. Those were my answers for the first twenty-nine years of my life.

Turning to these addictive substances, and many others, was my way of avoiding contact with God, Jesus, and any other spiritual being that might strike me down with lightning because I was such a bad girl. I was constantly terrified. My soul was empty. There were people in my life—family, friends, teachers, coaches, co-workers—but I always felt alone. The only time I thought I was happy was when I was eating something "sinful," going out to get drunk, or obsessing over a new man in my life. That false happiness quickly faded when the sinful treat was finished, or my eyes opened to the hangover after a night of black-out drinking, or the man showed me how human he was. And then I was alone and empty again.

After many years of self-degradation and humiliation, I finally became sick and tired of being sick and tired. In a counseling session it was suggested to me that I just might need to get help for my addiction to food. That was the day my recovery from my addictions, and more importantly, my relationship with my higher power (God) began. For some strange reason, I was struck open-minded and willing.

I may never know why my heart and soul opened to God at that point in my life, but it really doesn't matter to me. What matters is that since then my relationship with God has been a comfort beyond anything I ever could have imagined. I find refuge in my daily communion with Him and I have faith in His guidance. I turn to Him in gratitude and in sorrow. No matter what is happening in my life, I believe with all my heart that He is right by my side, caring for me and loving me every step of the way.

I didn't come to this new-found faith overnight, but instead through a daily commitment to improving myself through self-examination and adherence to a few simple principles presented to me by others who were experiencing recovery from addictions. I had to heal physically and emotionally through eating a healthy diet, avoiding alcohol and drugs, and experiencing a whole lot more counseling with qualified professionals. It took years of living clean and sober before I could even think of investigating my spirituality.

One of the many things that aids my daily commitment to recovery and growth is the use of structured literature, written by other recovering addicts, spiritual and religious leaders, and the like. There are not enough words in the world for me to express my appreciation for all those who have taken the time to share their spiritual journey through writing. So, I offer only this volume of daily readings from my own journey as a gift back to the world. It is my experience and my experience only, for that is all I can honestly share with anyone today.

May the words that follow help you in your spiritual journey—whatever that may be.

Believing Is Seeing

The power of God. Love. Miracles.

It used to be that I had to have proof to believe in something. I had to be able to lay my hands on something to say that it existed. I couldn't imagine recognizing true love without a bouquet of flowers or a wedding ring. I thought miracles were something someone made up to give people hope where there was none. And God's power, if it was real, was too important to help me.

Something changed for me when I set aside all my previously conceived notions and started asking others for help. In trusting the people around me to guide me on my path in life, I started to see that my belief in them and their experiences was giving me hope. I realized that I didn't need any proof to believe what I already felt in my heart.

TODAY: I will remember that because I believe, I see more clearly.

January 2 — My Attitude Is The Key

For the longest time—twenty-nine years to be exact—I lived my life chained to my addictions to food and alcohol, as well as all the unhealthy behaviors and beliefs those addictions produced. I thought the whole world was against me, that my lot in life was unfair and I should be pitied. I blamed everything and everyone around me for my unhappiness, never knowing that the foundation of all my problems came from deep within myself.

Once I put down the food and alcohol and started to take a look at how I acted on a daily basis, and how I reacted to what went on around me, I realized that no thing or person could make me feel or be a certain way. In other words, I was responsible for my own contentment. I was responsible for my own behaviors. It became clear to me that how I reacted—or didn't react—to things said to me or done to me, would be the catalyst to my mood for the rest of the day. I learned a new way of looking at life which became the key to a peaceful heart.

Today: I will remember that my attitude is the key to my happiness or unhappiness. Which door will I unlock today?

Awareness

I have always intended to be a good person. I never meant to bring pain or sorrow to the people around me. I wanted to be the best friend anyone ever had. Somehow, I always fell short. I hurt the ones I loved by things I said and did, and I betrayed friends through my selfish behaviors and attitudes. I argued with others over everything because I needed to prove that I knew more than anyone. All along, I was trying to be a fine, upstanding young lady, never realizing the path of destruction I was paving with my self-absorption and close-mindedness.

These days, a few years older and a bunch of days piled up since turning my back on my addictions, I have discovered that I don't have all the answers. I definitely make mistakes and sometimes say stupid things. Even in moments when I am hoping to help someone else, how that person perceives my actions may hurt their feelings. The difference between the old me and the new me is that today I am able to see when I have harmed another or made a mistake, and I am able to admit to it and amend for it. Most importantly, I am open to trying again, even when I feel defeated.

Today: I will remember that while I may not be perfect, I do have many gifts to offer to the world. I will do what I can to help another today.

Living In Reality

As a child growing up in a dysfunctional home, I often lived in a world of fantasy. I pretended I was a princess locked in a castle's tower waiting for a knight in shining armor to save me. I pretended I was a famous actress being interviewed by Merv Griffin or Mike Douglas. I pretended I was the damsel in distress who was rescued by Ponch and Jon during an episode of C.H.I.P.S. In my mind, I very rarely lived in reality—it was just too hard.

Unfortunately, it became more and more difficult to maintain my fantasies without the addictive substances of food, alcohol, and drugs. In my teen years, I did what I could to get my hands on the next fix, and in my early twenties, I lived my life for the binges and the black-outs that followed. It was all I could do to escape the reality of myself—a fearful, self-absorbed, and suspicious girl who cared only about what the world owed her.

My recovery from my addictions only began when the fantasy of control was smashed. I had to admit and accept that I was truly powerless over the things that I was putting into my body to obtain escape. Not only was I powerless over those substances, but I was also powerless over escaping reality. To grow in my recovery, I not only had to accept reality, but I also had to live in it. It has not always been easy, but with the help and guidance of all those who have gone before me, I have discovered that reality is the only place I want to be today.

Today: I will remember that looking for an escape from whatever it is I need to face is the first step to stunting my progress. Instead, I will embrace my fears and use them as an opportunity to grow.

What Yesterday Meant

JANUARY 5

My past is what it is, and there is nothing I can do to change that. For me to sit in judgment of my former self, my younger self, or the person I once was is for me to close my eyes to the beauty of the growth that has occurred in me as I have walked my path in life. To do so would be to judge God and His plan for me.

Instead, I can express my gratitude to some of the memories of my yesterdays. Because of them, I am able to avoid hurting the feelings of those with whom I come in contact. I can see where my voice needs to be heard and where my silence, instead, will give comfort. I can respect the moments that have brought me to tears by trusting others to guide me through difficult times, instead of trying to deal with my sadness alone. Today, I often find out what yesterday meant.

I embrace what has passed and how I have been. Those things have helped to form me into the woman I am today—and the woman I am today is someone I like.

TODAY: I will remember that the past is a wonderful tool with which to measure my growth.

January 6

Service Spreads Joy

When I was in my teens and walking around forlorn and unhappy, my mother would suggest that I try volunteering for something. She said that helping others might make me feel better about myself. That made no sense to me at the time. All I could think about was who was going to help me—who was going to take care of me?

Today, I know for certain that a huge part of my place here on earth is to help others. Whether that means volunteering at a local hospital to visit patients, raising money for cancer research, speaking respectfully to the wait staff at a fancy function I'm attending, or simply living a life that may inspire someone else, it is something for which I am responsible every day of my life.

How my service to others spreads, I often don't know. But what I do know is this: When I knocked over a display at the grocery store yesterday and was on my hands and knees putting it back into place, my day was brightened significantly by the woman I had never met before who stopped her own shopping to help me.

Today: I will remember that even if I am not recognized for it, my service to others will never go unappreciated.

Getting Real With God

Where's the proof that there is a God? Has anyone ever given you any concrete evidence to convince you that a supreme being exists? Isn't it silly to pray to someone or something that might not even be there?

My whole life, I have been taught to pray. From Sunday school to confirmation classes and weekly church services, I have been told what prayers are best for certain situations in life. No one ever proved to me that God was listening, they just said He was, and I believed them—maybe because they were older than I was, or maybe because not believing scared me too much. But none of that ever really worked for me.

Through recovery from my addictions, I have learned to "fake it until I make it." I learned to pray even when I felt like God wasn't there, but to be honest with Him as to what was in my heart. After being assured by others that I would not be struck by lightning if I questioned Him, I was able to get real with God. It has been those personal discussions I have had with God that have helped me the most. The times when I have gone to Him out of desperation and have shared my feelings with Him through honestly speaking or writing what was in my heart have been the times when I have felt the most relieved and peaceful.

Skeptics may scoff and say that without proof they can't believe and therefore, they won't waste time praying. For me, I don't need proof. Some days, prayer is all I've got.

TODAY: I will remember that finding my way to God is as simple as sharing a cup of coffee and good conversation with a friend.

January 8

Laugh A Little... Or A Lot

Is there anything better than a laughing fit that comes up in the middle of a crying jag? I can feel as though I'm in a hopeless situation, with no idea where to turn or how to make things better, when all of a sudden something silly or inane happens and I find myself smirking, maybe even giggling, or laughing out loud.

To me, there is nothing better than a good laugh. It fills my soul with a strength that comes only through letting go. Because when I am laughing, I have given up control. I have surrendered to something greater than my pain, and much more nourishing than my worry and self-pity.

Most of all, I truly enjoy laughing at myself—my little idiosyncrasies, my obsessive-compulsive nature, my graceless way of tripping on flat sidewalks, or walking into parking meters and park benches. I am, without a doubt, funny.

Today: I will throw my head back and laugh out loud—and I will have hope.

Using Pain To Grow

January 9

Pain is a funny thing. When I'm standing in it, I want no part of it. But once it becomes a thing of my past, I can look back on it and feel gratitude for the lessons it taught me.

As a child, I grew up in a dysfunctional home, was the victim of child and sexual abuse, and was taught to fear the almighty, punishing hand of God. Through the help of professional counselors and spiritual guides, I have been able to look the pain of the past in the eye, understand it, accept it, and let go of it. The path wasn't always easy, but it remains the most cherished time of my adult life. As I put down the crutches of food, alcohol, men, and rationalization, the little girl who survived that childhood trauma began smiling. Through self-honesty and trust in those who have helped me to find my way, I can now walk beside that little girl, holding her hand and laughing with her, the way little girls do.

Since facing the pain of the past, life is much easier, but every day isn't a bowl of cherries. Pain and fear often continue to cross in front of me. But today I can walk through them, knowing that they will not last forever, and that a valuable lesson may be learned because of them. That in itself is enough to keep me moving forward.

Today: I will remember that growth through pain is to be welcomed, not avoided.

Go Ahead And Stumble

Have you ever been taking a walk, breathing in the fresh air, soaking in the warm sun, and enjoying the tweeting of little birds, when... trip!... suddenly you are stumbling forward, trying to keep yourself from landing face-first on the sidewalk?

As I follow my path in life, I often find myself trying to maintain some semblance of dignity, and hoping I won't look like a complete idiot when "they" realize that I have no idea what's going on around me. It sometimes feels like I was absent the day life's rule book was handed out in school. Everyone around me seems to know how to act, when to laugh and when not to, and what they want out of life, while I bumble through conversations and laugh out loud as the room suddenly goes silent.

How often I have found that when I compare what I feel about myself to how other people "appear" to me, I always come up short. How can I possibly know what thoughts are running through the mind of my boss as he "brilliantly" presents our new findings to the board of directors? How can I guess what feeling is pulsing through the soul of my best friend as she "calmly" applies a band-aid to her son's bloody knee? Perhaps in his mind, my boss's presentation isn't "brilliant," but instead mind-numbingly boring. And, maybe my best friend's "calmness" is really concern that she isn't good enough at being a mom.

I have yet to meet anyone in my travels who hasn't felt like a fool on more than one occasion. We all walk along, bumbling, stumbling, dazed, and confused most of the time. The reality is that we were all absent from school on the day they handed out life's rule book.

TODAY: I will remember that tripping is all part of being human.

What God Wants

January 11

I spent way too much time fearing the vengeful hand of God that I remember learning about as a child. I was convinced that any thought that ran through my mind about how I would like to be, would be one that God kept from me.

Several years ago, I was walking through the heartache of a broken relationship. In my thirties and never having been married, I was once again sure that God was keeping from me what I truly wanted: a loving marriage with the man of my dreams. I began to believe that He wanted me to be single so that I would have more time to do His work and carry His message. And while I was at a time in my life when I genuinely wanted to follow God's will, I worried that if this was it, I would never be truly happy.

I shared this fear with a trusted friend over coffee, a box of tissues, and many tears. Her response to my fear was one that I have carried in my heart every moment since. She said, "Jessica, if it is what God wants for you, He'll make you want it, too."

Today: I will remember that my heart will always be filled with peace when I am following God's will.

January 12

Being Honest With Myself

Ignorance is bliss. Whoever said that was a genius, right? It is much easier to walk through life not knowing when my behavior has upset someone or when something I've said has hurt the feelings of a loved one. I can rest easy at night when I don't recognize where and when I have been selfish or close-minded. When I deny my shortcomings, I think I'm a pretty cool character.

But, the more I ignore the things I don't like about myself, the more I withdraw from reality. While it isn't easy to look within myself to find the answers to the discomfort I often feel, it is worth every ounce of energy it takes. Only when I acknowledge that which limits my growth can I amend my behaviors and thoughts and move beyond them, slowly becoming the person I am meant to be.

Ignorance is fear. Fear of change. Fear of truth. Fear of the unknown. Left alone, it will provide for me only superficial relationships and an empty soul. However, if I push beyond it and welcome self-honesty, I can open the doors to fulfilling friendships and continuous personal growth.

Today: I will remember that being honest with myself about who I am is the first step to becoming a better person.

Saved By The Rescue

January 13

Before I found recovery from my addictions, I ventured out to an animal shelter to adopt a cat. A friend talked me into it, telling me that having a kitten would make living alone seem less lonely. What I didn't know when I picked out the tattered and dirty little ball of white and brown fur was that she would one day save my life.

As my addiction progressed and my life began to spiral into a mess of uncontrolled eating, drinking, and selfish behavior, I withdrew into myself more and more. The danger of that for me was that I hated myself, and since I was often all alone, I lived in a constant state of hatred and anger. I decided the world would be a better place without me and that the only thing left for me to do was go on one final binge and then kill myself.

As I sat on my sofa, deciding how and where I would take my own life, my cat pranced into the center of my living room. She stopped and sat facing me. In that moment, I knew she knew what I was thinking. And, strangely enough, I knew she needed and loved me—even in my sickness and selfishness. She was the closest thing to God I had in my life, and in that moment, He used her to save me. While it took a few more months of desperation for me to reach out for help with my addictions, that was truly the last time I thought of killing myself. It was no longer an option.

Eleven years later, that dear soul jumps up on my lap when I'm watching television and pushes her nose past whatever I'm reading so I'll cradle her in my arms. I look down at her and as I listen to her soft purr, my heart swells. And as I stroke the soft fur of her back, my prayer is one of gratitude. My meditation is one of hope.

Today: I will remember that God speaks to me and comforts me through all creatures, great and small.

January 14

Expose The Sickness

Alone with my thoughts is very often not a safe place to be. It starts slowly, with just a tiny corner of my mind questioning something I've said or done, but within minutes it can become a monster with tentacles reaching into all the dark places I have ever experienced. It yanks on the low self-esteem of my childhood, the shame of my years in active addiction, or the fear that has taken so much from me by paralyzing me. It tells me that whatever I have said, done, or thought was selfish and wrong.

My defense against it is giving myself a voice—either through talking to someone else that I trust and sharing my feelings, or putting pen to paper and writing a letter to God, or myself, or the person with whom I've most recently had an uncomfortable encounter or conversation. Once I have a voice, the monster inside my head begins to fade back and the song of recovery becomes a bit clearer. I listen to the voice on the other end of the phone and remember that I have matured in how I deal with others and in how I behave. I read the words I have written on paper and see my diseased mind trying to coax me back into self-righteousness and close-mindedness. I discover my truth by stepping outside of my mind.

Today: I will remember the phrase I once heard shared in a recovery meeting: "My mind is like a bad neighborhood; I should never go there alone."

Anger Is A Liar

January 15

It stings to be hurt by harsh words from someone I love. It is humiliating to have a co-worker or friend point out a mistake I've made. After the initial moment of self-degradation, I sit and stroke my anger, envisioning my revenge. I can almost feel the pain I will inflict with my words and actions, as I gather my resentments and rationalize what I will do to "get even." My anger gives me a false sense of power and courage. The key word in the previous sentence is "false."

While there is nothing wrong with feeling angry, acting on my anger before thinking is rarely a good idea. Anger blinds me from reality and tells me the feelings of other people don't matter. It drives me to lash out at another, instead of reaching out to another. It gives me an excuse to behave poorly, instead of doing my best to act with grace and dignity. The momentary "boldness" that I feel in anger almost always becomes "reckless" in its manifestation.

Today: I will remember to stop and be still before I speak or act on my anger.

JANUARY 16

The Real Me

It used to be that I spent my time in relationships trying to be the person I thought my partner wanted me to be. Whether it was a love relationship, a friendship, or a co-worker, I thought I could make everyone like me by being who they wanted me to be. The problem with that philosophy is that I had to spend my life lying. I had to act as if I agreed with opinions that weren't my own. I had to hide my true feelings about certain things for fear of being "found out" or "exposed" for who I wasn't. I was pretending to be someone I wasn't. Inevitably, the lies rose to the surface and the relationships in my life came to an end, one by one.

Today, I have learned that being in a relationship isn't always easy. Sometimes I am going to disagree with my husband, friend, or co-worker. I may become fearful of losing someone close to me by being honest about my feelings. But whatever the situation is today, and even if all my fears rise to the surface because of it, I know I must be honest or the relationship will never stand a chance. I know this because in order to love myself, I had to know the real me. I had to look deep within to discover who I have been, who I am today, and who I would like to be—warts and all. If I want anyone else to love me, I have to become vulnerable to them seeing me in exactly that same way.

TODAY: I will remember that being respectfully honest about who I am and how I feel is a sure way to enhance my relationships.

Simple Choice

I take a look at my life today and I ask myself: have I truly been living or merely existing? Have I been enjoying each day, accomplishing tasks with purpose, or because I am expected to and feel I must? Am I laying my head down on the pillow at night with a sense of freedom and peace, or with exhaustion and desire for escape from reality through sleep?

If I don't like my answers, it is my choice whether or not I change. I can stop running and face whatever it is that scares me, learn from it, and grow. I can walk away from behaviors that keep me chained to my disease of addiction and tendency to self-destruct. I can make the choice to reach for the goal that has always been just a far-away fantasy in my mind.

For this day I know that it really is a simple choice.

TODAY: I will remember that if I am not truly living, I am merely dying.

JANUARY 18

The Mask of Rationalization

I can make anything sound okay with a good rationalization: I cut off that guy on the highway because I needed to get to my appointment on time; I only called my co-worker a bitch because she is one—someone has to be honest with her or she'll never change; I deserve to go out and get drunk, because it's been a tough week.

The problem with rationalizations is that they really only serve to justify an unattractive behavior of which I am not proud. In addition, they often have a hurt, angry, or annoyed person on the other end of them. And as long as I believe my rationalizations, I am stuck.

It is difficult to admit that I am sometimes a selfish person who doesn't treat others as kindly as I would like to be treated. I don't want to recognize that I turn to my vices when the going gets tough. The failure to accept my defects of character is, in itself, a character limitation. I know that there will be no growth for me until I set aside rationalizing who I am or how I act for a true desire to recognize my faulty behaviors and ask for help in changing them.

TODAY: I will remember that rationalizations can be hurtful. I pray to set aside the mask of rationalizations and accept myself and my life as it truly is.

The Two "A"s

Acceptance and appreciation are two things that assist greatly in building a strong relationship. Whether it be with a family member, friend, co-worker, or soul mate, the two "A"s can be the best possible guarantee to growing in love and trust with another.

When I accept someone, I don't expect them to change. I speak to them with respect for who they are today, without hinting or nudging that they could improve themselves "if they would only..." And when I appreciate someone, I notice their good qualities. I point out their actions that have touched my heart and made my day a little better. The two "A"s are a beautiful way to live and interact with others. So why are they so difficult to remember on a daily basis?

I believe it is human nature to be concerned with one's self before others. Therefore, it takes a willingness to become aware of how I speak to and behave towards those with whom I interact daily. After I become aware, I must then begin to change my expectations of others and how I believe they should be. I must recognize the good qualities they exude, instead of sitting in judgment of their shortcomings. And, finally, I need to verbalize my appreciation to those who show kindness, love, and acceptance back to me. It can be a tall order—especially during times when I am sitting in self-pity or loneliness. But the end result of the two "A"s is always worth any amount of energy I must put into applying them.

Today: I will remember that each person is a child of God, and living exactly the way he or she is meant to be living today. I will also remember that saying "thank you" goes a long way.

The Gift Of Desperation

Desperation can be a beautiful thing. Many times it is the catalyst for change that so many people need to move forward in their lives. For me, the desperation was a wall of fat that sat between me and you, between me and God. It was a bottle of wine that glazed over the pain and shame of yesterday and kept me petrified. It was a dark cloud of memories that hovered over my head, taunting and haunting me. The desperation of life made it clear to me that it was time for a change, or time to put an end to it all with a bottle of pills.

The first step of change was terrifying, and yet brought about relief I never knew existed. Just admitting to another person that I needed help gave me freedom from the desperation. Fortunately, that feeling of freedom helped to carry me through the fear of learning and embracing an entirely new way of living. With each trembling step, it was important to remind myself where I had been and how desperately I did not want to go back there. I had to have faith that the next step would move me forward, into the life I was truly meant to live—whatever that was.

I believe what is most difficult about change is the not knowing. As I change my behaviors in relationships and with the world around me, I have no idea what kind of response I will receive. As I begin to trust in a Power greater than myself, I let go of my ideas of what my life should be and step into the day not knowing what will be next. To remain in change, which is to grow and learn, I must keep taking each next step—no matter how scary it may seem.

TODAY: I will remember that each step forward brings me closer to the person I am meant to be. I will face my fears of the unknown future and learn about myself and the world as I go.

To Feel Is To Love

Have you ever tried not to laugh when you found something amusing? Have you noticed that trying not to laugh just makes you laugh harder? And when you've tried to hold back tears in public because you don't want to be embarrassed, don't they flow from your eyes anyway?

Our feelings are the core of our being. They carry us through each moment of each day. Whether it is an inner joy we feel as we watch the sun rise first thing in the morning, or sadness when we pass a dead deer on the side of the road, each feeling we experience makes us whole.

It's okay to cry at movies or laugh out loud when you trip on the sidewalk. It's okay to love, to fear, to hope, to tolerate, to dread, to accept. Whatever we're feeling at any given moment is okay. It is what we do with those feelings that is important.

If my feelings are bothering me, I write them down or talk to a trusted friend about them. Sometimes, I will even write a letter to God, telling Him everything I'm feeling and asking Him to help me move beyond it.

And if my feelings are of gratitude, I also share them—with others and with God. For I know it is true that nothing good inside of me will ever sprout wings if I leave it locked in my heart.

Today: I will share my feelings, appropriately, with someone I trust.

January 22

If I Were Any Different Than I Am Right Now, I'd Be Worried

Some days are better than others. It's when I'm sitting in one of "the others" that I tend to beat myself to a pulp for being sad, or bitchy, or obsessive-compulsive to the nth degree. I tell myself that I have been through years of counseling and should be better by now. I reprimand myself for marinating in self-pity when things don't go my way. I become so uncomfortable in my own skin that I secretly wish I could shed it like a snake and become someone brand new!

And then I remember where I have come from. I remember the obstacles of pain, abuse, and fear that littered the beginning of my life's journey. I remember the strength and courage it took to face all that garbage and work my way through cleaning it up, one piece at a time. I remember all the people that God put in my life to help me along the way. And I remember how much those people cared for me and accepted me, even when I was sad, bitchy, obsessive-compulsive, and sitting in self-pity. They knew that those defects I was so eager to shed were once tools of survival, plain and simple. They helped me to recognize them and appreciate the strength they once gave to me. And they helped me to find ways to let go of them.

They also cautioned me to the fact that occasionally, as I walk through the days ahead, some of those defects will creep back onto my path from time to time. How I act and react to their reappearance will determine whether they bounce off of me or stick to me like gum on the bottom of my shoe.

Today: I will remember that some days are better than others, and that's all there is to it.

Fear Is Opportunity

January 23

Sometimes I am so afraid of something that I become petrified. I fear the answer to a request I want to make to my boss, so I just don't ask. I fear my manuscript will be rejected, so I stop writing it. I fear the rollercoaster will fly off the track, so I sit and watch as others enjoy the ride.

I could go on forever, listing my fears and denying the parts of life they cause me to miss. Instead, I choose to face them—to conquer them. Someone once told me that F.E.A.R. stands for "Face Everything And Recover." For me, that means that each time I am presented with a fear, I am also presented with an opportunity. If I face the fear, stand up to it, and walk through it, I will recover a little bit more of myself that I have lost to all the fears of my past. As I walk through it, I will know that the next time I am faced with it, I will be able to do it again, with an even greater confidence. I will even gain valuable experience that I may someday be able to share with another, perhaps adding a tiny bit of hope to their world.

Today, I choose to live. I choose to breathe in the beauty of God's world and open my heart to relationships with others on this life's journey. I choose to laugh and be amazed, to throw my hands in the air and scream at the top of my lungs as the roller coaster plunges down that hauntingly steep hill. And, if you are afraid, I choose to hold your hand so we can walk through your fear together.

Today: I will remember that living can be scary sometimes, but that watching as life goes by is more terrifying than anything I might find in the dark.

JANUARY 24

Accepting The Rope

When I have cried so much and for so long that there are no tears left, I have reached despair. When I stare blankly into space, no fantasies of better days ahead left to occupy my mind, I have only misery. When I think the world would be a better place without me, I have lost hope.

It is in this pit of depression and emptiness that I recognize my weakness. Grabbing for what I want in life, ignoring the needs of those around me, swallowed by my own desire for more—I, alone, am nothing.

I stand in the dark with two choices: I can crumble in this pit of despair or I can shout out for help. If I crumble, I will become lost in the legions of dirt and grime around me. If I shout out, my only job will be to accept whatever rope is lowered down into the pit, grab onto it, and allow it to guide me wherever it may.

For me, it is only when I am truly desperate that I am able to accept that rope—even when it's not the one I think I should be given. It is only through that pit of misery that I am able to accept, with blind faith, whatever guidance has been offered.

TODAY: I will remember to be grateful for my most desperate moments.

No Returns

January 25

For a million dollars, I would not want to go back and relive my childhood. Like so many others in this world, I grew up in a dysfunctional home, ruled by my father's alcoholism. I was abused—physically, sexually, and emotionally. Worst of all, I lived in a constant state of fear that I would burn in Hell because God hated me. That said, there is nothing in this world that could make me want to change any of it.

That may sound a little insane to most people, and when I was living in my disease of addiction, I would have concurred. I dreamed of a childhood that included a Brady Bunch family that loved and adored me.

Then, when I found recovery, I also found people who were trained to guide me through those painful memories toward healing. To face the pain of abuse, and walk through the feelings of abandonment and self-loathing that would often creep into my life and shatter my days was horrifying—and yet, so empowering. And as I pushed past my fear of God and found the power that guides and comforts, rather than punishes, I realized that my past—every moment of it—is a gift not to be returned. What happened on the other side of that pain helped me to realize the strength within, the hope that never dies, and the person I was always meant to be.

Today: I will remember that every single moment in my life is valuable to me. How I use it to my benefit or to my detriment is my choice.

JANUARY 26

Simply Extraordinary

A butterfly haphazardly traveling through the air. The smell of honeysuckle on a hot, summer afternoon. The blonde curls that bounce with glee as my niece runs to greet me. Enchanted by these things, I stop to smile at the butterfly and recognize its grace. I breathe in God's aroma and remember long walks with my mom past the honeysuckle bushes near the high school, and I thank God for the joy that my sister's children bring me.

It is true that there are days when it becomes difficult for me to recognize and embrace the ordinary. I find myself becoming obsessed with finishing a project at work perfectly, and fail to notice the new bird's nest in the tree just outside my office window. I am hurt by something a friend has said, and I walk right by the bright yellow tulips that have just opened up to the world. Or, I forget how blessed I am with good health, and take for granted all the ordinary daily tasks that I can complete without assistance.

My life is extraordinary simply because it exists. Everything around me is extraordinary. When I fail to recognize this, I can be sure that I am focusing too much on myself and my wants, and not enough on the beauty and blessings of God's world.

TODAY: I will remember that each part of my day is extraordinary, if only I will open my eyes and soul to see it.

God's Will Is My Peace

Finding my way in this world is rarely easy. I look back over my life and see so many detours from the path—times when my selfish desires led me astray. I have wasted so much time chasing after fame, Prince Charming, a perfect body, and anything that would make me feel better. And I have always been disappointed.

Awakened from my selfish obsessions through recovery from addiction, my heart became open for the first time to God's will. I welcomed Him into my soul and recognized the joy that would come from surrendering fully to His path for me. Filled with peace, I have moved on and accepted His grace—on most days.

For I am human, and I often slide backward into myself and my obsessions. Yet, I am consistently amazed at God's ability to awaken me when I am hypnotized by my own egotism and selfishness. His methods never fail and I find myself humbled in ways that strengthen me rather than humiliate me.

Today: I will remember to walk with God on life's journey, rather than trying to lead the way.

Hunger Check

When I'm empty inside, I search for something—anything—to fill that emptiness. Will it be a large pizza with extra cheese or a jug of apple wine? Will it be the perfect man or the job that finally recognizes my outstanding work? Perhaps it will be the cult leader who offers me the fantastic kool-aid journey to never-never land.

The emptiness that once led me to reach out for my addictions now warns me of impending danger on the path ahead. My emptiness is a soul sickness, not an imagined void or black hole. It is my human belief that I must "go it alone" or "find my own way." It is my lack of communion with my higher power.

Today: I will remember that my hunger—whether physical, emotional, or spiritual—is a signal to check my diet, my motives, and my relationship with God.

Hope Received Is Hope Given

January 29

As I have walked through life, day-by-day, I have been assisted by so many people. I can look back so far as to the man who was my softball coach when I was in third grade, and know that his encouragement of my talents on the field gave me hope. There wasn't much during that time that rendered me hopeful, so the value he put in my abilities to pitch and bat and run the bases is something that fills my heart with gratitude, even today, thirty-plus years later.

What I have recognized on the other side of hope—giving it—has filled not only my heart, but also my soul, with an energy that propels me through each day. When I share a heartache with a friend or tell my story to another recovering addict, my purpose abounds without my even knowing how far it will reach. To give a sense of hope to someone who can't see beyond the sadness of the moment or even grasp the idea that things may be better one day is a treasure for both the person who receives, as well as the person who gives.

Today: I will remember that someone has always been put in my path to give me hope. To whom can I be of service in that way today?

Be A Fan

As a kid, I hung posters of movie stars on the walls of my room. I saved up my allowance to buy the newest Barry Manilow album each year. I watched General Hospital every day after school. I was a fan, for sure.

From time to time, we all need distractions, something to take our mind away from the reality of our lives. Going to the theater to see your favorite actor perform lets you escape into a fantasy world when real life is just too hard. Making sure you're at the bookstore the day your favorite author's next hardcover novel is revealed gives you something to look forward to when life is boring. And how wonderful is the sense of belonging when you hold season tickets to the best sports team on earth?

My family is certainly dysfunctional. When we get together, there is often a great tension that hangs in the air. We all try to avoid sliding back into the diseased roles of our past and many times say and do stupid things. But when the topic of New York Giants football comes up, that all goes away. The one thing we all agree on is that we are crazy-in-love with the Giants—we always have been, and we always will be.

TODAY: I will remember to appreciate the fanaticism in the world around me. Whether it is a body covered in tattoos or a lady with twenty cats, it is something to believe in.

Finding A Way To Love

January 31

Anger is so strong a word—hard and powerful. Hatred wraps itself around our hearts and squeezes until we literally feel the pain in our guts, in a stiffening of our necks, in the pulsing blood flow to our temples. Without some sort of tending to, anger and hatred will kill us—physically by way of heart attack, stroke or the like; emotionally by telling us the whole world is against us; and spiritually by blocking any path with which God may reach us.

It is only through finding a way to love that we are able to let go of that anger and hatred. Whether it be by visiting a therapist or psychologist to face the anger and hatred of our pasts, attending a religious service regularly to open the lines of communication with the God of our understanding, or amending for our harms toward others through an honest self-appraisal, it is imperative that we allow love to enter our hearts.

For some of us, the love rolls in like the low tide on a warm summer evening, calmly caressing our pains and sadness away. For others, it is a tidal wave that lifts us up to a power of enlightenment that we never even knew existed. Either way, it is worth it!

Today: I will remember to face my anger and hatred head on. I will reach out for help to walk through it and move beyond it, so my heart can embrace the love that is all around me.

February 1

Pain And Fear Are Not Unique

When I look back over my life and recognize the mistakes I've made, the stupid things I've said, and the mean things I've done to others, I see that all of it came to be because of a fear in my heart that told me I wasn't good enough or pretty enough or talented enough. The pain of my past only helped to validate that fear, reminding me that they will laugh at me, or he will leave, or she will betray me.

After many years of searching for a way to remove these painful memories and the fears that come with them, I found that only through a relationship with God am I able to overcome such intense feelings. Furthermore, I have found that in this pain and fear, I am not unique. The majority of people are walking around with their own set of painful memories and fearful thoughts. They, too, are saying and doing things that may seem outlandish or spiteful to others, but to themselves, they are simply surviving, and for some, trying to thrive in a world that is "out to get them."

There will be times when I will get caught in the crossfire of someone else's painful moments. How I react to their behavior will either add to their fear, providing them more proof of a harsh and unfair world, or it will erase some of the pain by allowing them to be human. The choice is mine to make.

Today: I will remember that every person's journey is filled with moments of pain and fear. What others say and do is not a reflection on me, but on them.

Guard Against Darkness

When someone is in need, do I rush to their side and offer assistance, or do I turn away, pretending I don't see? As I walk toward an entrance, do I stop to open the door for the elderly woman behind me, or do I walk through hastily, ignoring her tired, aged movements so I can get to my appointment on time? Do I attend the funeral of a co-worker's husband, or do I choose to use work as an excuse to avoid her anguish?

Whatever I do today in response to another person's pain is my gift to God. Whatever I do today to make another person's day just a little bit brighter is my gift to humanity. Whatever I do today to guard against the darkness is my gift to myself. Whether it be helping someone find an item in the supermarket, thanking the guy who puts the new windshield wipers on my car, or calling a friend I haven't heard from in a while to ask how she's doing, I am guarding against the darkness.

TODAY: I will remember that with each selfless act, I not only brighten the day of another, but also my own.

FEBRUARY 3

Imagination Protects, Then Creates

As a child, I spent many hours escaping into my imagination. I left the physical and emotional bruises of that day's beatings behind as I traveled into the corners of my mind—corners that held forests full of lions and bears and tigers, all sent to protect me, the princess of their kingdom. They surrounded me and growled at predators, scaring them away before they could even come close to hurting me. They watched over me while I slept peacefully, shielding me from the dangers of the night. They ran with me through the trees to waterfalls surrounded by bright yellow and pink and orange flowers that bloomed only in my presence. And they all loved me because I brought life and hope to all the dark places in their empire.

That imagination protected the soul of the little girl who was abused and ignored. It rocked her to sleep at night and carried her through moments of terror that might otherwise have shattered the sanity of her mind. It allowed her to know her own beauty, if only for a few moments. And it kept her from dying when all the world seemed too dark for life.

Today, that imagination creates rather than protects. It glides through reality rather than running from it. And it rejoices in the life that was saved because of it.

TODAY: I will remember to appreciate the gift of my imagination.

Worriers Miss Out

February 4

What if I don't get the job? How long will it be until I meet my soul-mate? Should I stay or go? Can you believe how they treated me?

The worries of a day, a week, a month, or a year can keep my mind spinning indefinitely. I can gnaw on a bothersome concern or go over an unfortunate situation in my mind for hours, trying to figure out how it could have been improved—or better yet—how I can keep it from ever happening again. And, as I gnaw and gnash my way through a day with worry, I miss my life. I miss moments of joy and serenity, pleasure and pain.

When I focus on the moment instead of yesterday's mistake or tomorrow's potential fumble, I get through it. In fact, I do more than get through it. When I focus on the moment, I enjoy it and grow from it. I let go of the need for control and accept the brush of truth against my soul. My heart opens to feelings and I can learn from what I see, hear, and touch. When I allow life's embrace, I blossom from it.

Today: I will remember to let it go, whatever it is, and just live—just for today.

FEBRUARY 5

Don't Run Away–Move Beyond

So often throughout my life, I have thought of running away. I have wished that I could go somewhere in the world where no one knows me, or my family, or what I have done in my past. I could have started fresh, and been the person I always knew I could be. With no scars and no past to avoid talking about, I could have been a kind, generous, and loving person to everyone I met along the way.

What I have learned from some of the physical moves that I have made in my life—to begin my college education, to start a new job, and simply to go on a long vacation—is that I always take me with me. And when I take me with me, that includes taking my family, my memories, and all the things I have done in my past with me as well. There is no escape from what has already happened, from what I have already done.

From these lessons, I now know that the only way to become the person I have always known I can be is to face the reality of myself instead of running from it. Through self-discovery and self-acceptance, I have grown to understand my past, my motives, and the behaviors of my dysfunctional family. This has enabled me to move beyond the person who was stuck in addiction and into a new world of recovery. Instead of running from the past, I can shed the baggage of shame and guilt I have been carrying, and take along only the lessons I have learned from it, with no regrets.

TODAY: I will remember that running from a problem will only give me more luggage to carry on my journey. For today, I choose to take along only a carry-on bag of wisdom.

Discomfort Is A Warning

February 6

There are days when I feel like I can't do anything right. I think bad thoughts about others or selfishly ignore the needs of those around me. I procrastinate at work by playing computer games or gossiping with my office neighbor. I forget to talk to God, asking Him to guide my words, thoughts, and actions.

Throughout those days, I often feel uncomfortable in my skin. Sometimes I know why, other times I just know I don't feel quite right. That's where the rubber meets the road for me. When the feeling of discomfort with myself has settled in, it is a warning. I can heed that warning and take action. I can sit down and write out an inventory of my day, checking my behaviors and motives. I can call a trusted friend and share that inventory honestly. I can turn my thoughts to God in prayer, and ask for guidance and forgiveness.

Part of what is beautiful about my life today is that I know and accept that I am a human being. I am going to make mistakes, and I am going to sometimes revert back to unhealthy behaviors. The difference today is that I have a choice as to whether or not I stay in the discomfort.

Today: I will remember that how I feel and how I act throughout each day can be a wonderful warning that I need to get in touch with God.

FEBRUARY 7

Explore The Fear

When I watch my cat explore the grocery bags I've just brought home from the store, I see the curiosity often attributed to our feline friends. I also see an air of vigilance as she sniffs each bag with caution and extreme care. She doesn't fear the new smells; she is simply intrigued by them and must discover for herself which bag deserves her attention. Even when the bag beside her suddenly falls over and she skitters out of the kitchen, she will always return to explore that which frightened her in the first place.

As I watch her, I think about how I approach new things in my life. More aptly put, I think about how I explore something that is outside of my comfort zone. Am I similar to my cat, who, bombarded by millions of outside scents, jumps into the middle of grocery bags and gets to work figuring out their potential? Or do I hide under the bed and wait for all that newness to be removed from what I already know: a bare kitchen floor?

Once again in life, I am reminded that fear often keeps me from taking chances, which then keeps me from discovering, learning, and growing.

TODAY: I will remember that taking chances may be scary, but if I'm willing to face the fear, I will always learn something from each chance I take.

Caution: Ego Straight Ahead

Just when I think I have it all together, when I believe I know the answers and am about to stick my chest out with pride—that's exactly when I need to take caution. The false confidence that comes with pride is one of the devil's greatest tricks on me. He preys on my egotism and lies in wait as I puff myself up with my own "greatness." How dangerous it is for me to play in that pool of elaborate self-image.

What usually happens when I feed into my ego is a sort of tripping over myself that is humiliating, rather than humbling. I speak when thinking I have the answers and sound like a fool. I walk with an air of arrogance and trip over a curb or run into a wall. I attempt to manipulate someone to do what I want and think is best for them, and end up hurting them, or worse, ruining a relationship.

The key to my true self-confidence is in remembering that of myself, I don't have anything together, and I don't know anything. My self-confidence is a gift from God. Along with humility, He grants me enough self-confidence to carry out my daily work and to share His love with others. It is when I forget that any power I have comes from God, that I give the devil an opening to my soul. And the devil does exist, waiting each moment of each day for my humiliation, my embarrassment, or my manipulative behaviors to lead me in his direction.

Today: I will remember that all that I am and all that I can do today is a gift from God.

Keep It Simple

These three words were part of the last conversation between the co-founders of Alcoholics Anonymous. Dr. Bob, who is famous for uttering this statement, knew that he had a tendency to complicate matters until they became so convoluted that a solution could rarely be found.

Most human beings, whether addicts or not, share this propensity to complicate things. Simple tasks become grand schemes. Committee meetings last for hours instead of minutes while members hash out ideas and opinions until everyone in attendance lacks the ability to care for the cause anymore. A quick report at work turns into spreadsheets and an unnecessary PowerPoint presentation.

My experience has shown me that when I turn my back on grandiosity, ego-inflation, and sticking my nose into business that isn't mine in the first place, my life becomes much simpler. I don't have all the answers. I don't always know what the best decision for the people around me is. In fact, I don't even know the best decision for myself the majority of the time. But I do know that if I stay focused on the simple pieces of each of my days—starting my day with prayer, reaching out to others to lend a hand, completing necessary tasks around my home and at work, taking care of myself—I will have peace.

Today: I will remember to keep it simple—whatever "it" is.

Being Responsible

There's no such thing as a free lunch. No pain, no gain. Freedom isn't free. So many of our contemporary slogans tell us that without a lot of sweat and tears there will be no success in life.

Most of us go through life trying to avoid feeling uncomfortable or doing things we don't want to do, like going to work every day or facing reality as it comes. We call in sick or show up and just go through the motions, or we sit in denial about defects within ourselves that are holding us back.

Through recovery from my addictions, I have learned that once I have embraced my job for what it is—a paycheck and a sense of daily stability—I am more adept at appreciating its worth in my life. And once I have stopped denying my defects of character, I am able to recognize the importance of working through them each day. My defects give me the opportunity to change and grow into the person God has always wanted me to be.

In essence, both my job and my defects have become daily resources from which I can gain experience and wisdom. The key is to find a way to be thankful for my job and face my character defects daily, in order to keep them from building up into an overwhelming pile of unwanted responsibilities and liabilities.

Today: I will remember that when I deny reality or procrastinate, I am simply guaranteeing a more difficult tomorrow.

February 11

Reacting With Self-Acceptance

As a child, I was often reminded by adults of the Golden Rule: "Do unto others as you would have them do to you." I learned that while others may be unkind, it is important that I treat everyone with kindness, which is how I would hope to be treated. Then in Sunday School, I learned the passage of the Bible (Matthew 5:38–40) that tells me that if I am slapped by another on my right cheek, I should turn to them the other cheek as well.

These two messages were hard to take when I was suffering through my own addiction, thinking the world was out to get me. If I was nice to people, wouldn't they take advantage of me? If I allowed others to harm me and continued to offer myself to them, wouldn't I be acting like a doormat? How was I to follow these suggestions when I truly believed the people around me were all against me?

Throughout my journey, I have learned that I teach others how to treat me by how self-accepting and self-respecting I am. In other words, I can be kind to others, but I can also set boundaries with the people in my life who may want to take advantage of my kindness, in order to take care of myself in the process.

What others may call me is their business. How I react to what they call me depends on my own self-acceptance.

Today: I will remember that how I feel about myself will reflect into all my relationships, whether with a long-time friend, or a stranger I pass on the street.

My Walk Is My Talk

There was a time in my life when I thought it was necessary for me to speak to others often and at great length about my opinions and beliefs. I had to make sure that people knew that I had the answers, that I was clear about the direction my life was taking, and that I was a good person. I told them about it all the time.

Life has gently shown me that how I act and what I do with my life are significantly more important than what I say or what I promise to do. The best way for me to show others how I would like to be treated is how I treat them. The best way to carry God's message of love is to be kind, accept differences, and give without expectation of return.

As Gandhi so beautifully put it, "My life is my message."

Today: I will remember that when I hear myself talking too much, it is a sign to check my actions.

I Can

I can talk myself out of anything! Too often, I find myself providing reasons why I shouldn't do something, or why I can't. It's too expensive to go to that retreat in Los Angeles; I don't have time to sit down and write every day, and besides, the chances of getting published are slim; I can't volunteer to be the treasurer of that group—I don't know a thing about money.

And, then there are the times when just like the "little engine that could," my positive attitude becomes my most important asset. Like when I began my journey of recovery and believed that because others were recovering, I could also recover; or when I decided to make time to write—whether published or not, the pursuit began to fill a hole in my soul.

I can make or break each day for myself through my perception of my own talents. "I can" speaks so much more positively than "I can't" or "it's too hard." Even if I fall down in the process of trying something, I can still get up and try again. I once heard it beautifully put when someone said, "Failure isn't falling down; it's staying down."

Today: I will remember that what I think of myself is extremely important to finding fulfillment in life.

Stop Hiding

For a very long time in my life, I hid from the world. Through addictions, a wall of fat, egotism, pride, and plain old-fashioned fear, I made up excuses and threw a cloak over the real me. I knew if you saw who I really was, you would laugh at me, you would run from me, you would hate me.

But when I was embraced by others who shared the same addictions before I was even able to admit my own powerlessness and defects, I was overcome with emotion. When people accepted my phone calls, I almost couldn't believe it. When those who had gone before me took time to sit and talk with me and share their experience, strength, and hope, I felt worthy for the first time in my life.

Through this acceptance, I was able to begin revealing more of myself to others. I could speak of things I had done or thought that I once vowed never to share. I could open my heart and mind to a new way of living because I saw that it worked for others in recovery. I began to want to be a person that loved others, instead of fearing them and hating them. I truly did crawl out of my hiding place—the consequence of which I can never fully explain, but of which I know deep down inside is a life of love.

Today: I will remember how it felt to be accepted and loved—just as I was—when I first began my journey of recovery. I will also remember that today I may be given the opportunity to give that same acceptance and love to someone else. I pray I will rise to the occasion.

February 15

I Am Not A Victim

I have spent a lot of time in my life blaming my circumstances, attitudes, and behaviors on others. I was overweight because my mom loved me by giving me certain sugary treats, and punished me by withholding dessert or other favorite foods. I was drunk all the time because my dad abused me as a child and I had to find some way to escape those horrible memories. I didn't trust anyone because I grew up in a dysfunctional family unit, where trust usually brought on hurt and disappointment.

I once was listening to a woman who was sharing about her own abusive childhood and she said, "You're a victim until you're eighteen; after that you're a volunteer." Ouch! That statement slapped me across the face. I realized that as a grown-up, I had to take responsibility for how I behaved and how I treated myself and others. I could no longer blame my parents or my childhood for my actions, or even for my close-minded beliefs about life and certain people.

This idea, while difficult to accept at first, has helped me to become a better person. In accepting responsibility for myself, I have begun to recognize certain behaviors that aren't so appealing. I have been able to ask others to help me find my way to a better me, and I have been able to let go of much of what the dysfunction of my childhood taught me. I no longer need to be chained to the past, or the pain of the past. I can be whoever I want to be.

Today: I will remember that how I behave today is a reflection on me, not my past. I will be responsible for myself and my actions.

I Need God's Help

February 16

Have you ever had one of those days when you feel like you're going to come right out of your skin? Sometimes there's no particular reason for it, but I can feel like my skin is crawling over and away from me, until it will leave me and I will explode into nothing. Those are the times when I know I need to rely on something outside of myself for sanity.

Through prayer, I can usually find some peace when I feel uncomfortable in myself. Whatever I'm doing, I stop and find a quiet place to talk to God—even if only for a few minutes. I ask Him to bless me with serenity. I pray for my mind to be still and my soul to be filled with His grace, rather than with my own fear and confusion.

Finally, I ask for God to grant me the faith to continue on through the day with patience and trust that He will change me. There is one thing I know for sure: that I alone cannot change how I feel. I need God's help.

Today: I will remember that I don't have to fight every feeling I have on my own. God is always there, waiting for me to reach out and ask for His help.

Not One Of Us Is Perfect

Growing up, I always wanted to be "worshipped." I wanted to be famous and have people look up to me. I wanted them to be impressed by me and wish they could know me.

I have come to learn that it is much more comfortable to be viewed by others as the person I really am. It is easier to be me when I am seen as a human being who has good and bad qualities, just like anybody else. With this realization, I have also learned that it is just as important to treat everyone I meet as a garden-variety human. How short sighted it has been of me to expect others to be perfect, when I know of my own limitations and humanness!

When I expect others to go about their business without disappointing me or hurting me, I am going to end up being resentful. Because this much is certainly true: we are all human beings and not one of us is perfect.

Today: I will remember that what I have often heard said is true: "Expectations are pre-meditated resentments."

Breathe AndKeep Going

February 18

Before I found recovery from my addictions, I experienced a kind of hell on earth. I was breathing and walking around, but I might as well have been dead. As I've written before, I thought about killing myself because of that misery, but I never tried. I just kept breathing.

Sometimes I wonder what happened to make that walking dead girl wake up. What was it that stunned her into awareness and got her to pay attention to the guidance of others and her higher power? The answer to the question doesn't even matter. What matters is that she kept going. She didn't try to kill herself. Her continuous breathing eventually got her to a place where she was finally fighting for herself, and was able to begin truly living.

Today, I learn from her. When things are rocky in my relationships or when I'm feeling stalled in my recovery process at work or in my creative life, I need to remember how that pre-recovery Jessica survived. She just kept going. Some days, that's enough for this Jessica, too.

Today: I will remember that just breathing is sometimes enough.

February 19

Act Toward Growth

What am I putting off today? From picking up the phone to reach out to someone, to sitting down to start writing that great American novel, it seems like there is always something that I am afraid of doing.

When I look back over my life, it is true that the things I most regret are the things I never did. I don't look back on the times I failed at something I tried and wrinkle my nose in disgust. But I do look back at the times I didn't do something out of the fear of failure—or the fear of success—and wish I had been strong enough at the time to try.

Studying abroad. Writing for the school newspaper. Applying for the internship that would have provided possible job opportunities. Asking that guy to dance. Offering my hand in friendship to the lonely new girl in school. These are things I look back on and feel an emptiness that will never be filled. I cannot go back and overcome the fear I felt during those times in my life. What I can do is remember the emptiness I feel when I think of them, and use it to propel myself into action the next time I am presented with an opportunity that stirs up some fear. I can act toward growth, rather than stay stuck in fear.

Today: I will remember that if I don't keep trying, my soul will be filled with empty regrets.

The Addiction Monster

February 20

Addiction is a horrible thing. As an addict, I have experienced more than one occasion where I have sworn off my substance and promised to change the way I lived my life. What inevitably happened was a phenomenon that I will never be able to explain. No matter how strong my resolve, I couldn't stop from picking up that substance—and once I picked it up, there was no way I could stop using it.

The guilt and shame that I felt from giving in to the substance then brought on the nasty me. I felt so bad about myself that I lashed out at everyone around me. I was so caught up in the addiction that I didn't even know I was hurting anyone. I truly believed that if I was hurting anyone, it was only myself.

Today I know for sure that the monster described so perfectly in the story of Dr. Jekyll and Mr. Hyde is truly the end result for me if I choose to pick up my addictive substance. I also know that the only way for me to keep from picking up my addictive substance is to ask for help, pray, share my story with someone else who is struggling, and remain humble—remembering always that my sobriety is a blessing from a power much greater than myself.

Today: I will remember that one sip, one bite, or one fix will only end up in one colossal mess. For today, I am willing to ask for help before I hand over the reins of my life to the monster that is my addiction.

My Bright Spot

This world can be a very dark place. The television, radio, internet, and newspapers all report the brutality of war and crime as if it is entertainment to our ears. We are constantly reminded of the selfishness of others and the inhumanity that exists around the globe and in our very own neighborhoods. It can become a daunting task to get out of bed and face the world for another day.

I may look at the news and the people around me and see only emptiness, fear, and hatred. But I must not allow myself to be pulled down into that pit of despair. I must carry the message of light that has been given so freely to me through my recovery from addiction. My job today is to "light up the darkness." I can smile and say thank you to the lady who hands me my change when I stop to get coffee before work. I can let someone out in front of me in traffic. I can leave an anonymous note of thanks on a co-worker's desk. I can call a friend just to tell her I'm grateful she's in my life today. I can hug my husband and tell him I love him—just because.

When I spend my day thinking of ways to brighten the world, I can stop worrying about the horrors going on around me.

Today: I will remember that something I do or say today may be the only lightness in someone's day.

Never Alone

February 22

For most of my life, I thought I had to "go it alone." I thought I was the only person I could count on. Everyone else had always let me down, so why trust? Why reach out and ask for help when my experience had always shown me that people will inevitably disappoint me?

Through the desperation that led me to recovery, I was forced to trust others. I had to rely on others to guide me through the program of recovery that had worked for them. I had to call on others to ask for help and to keep from turning back to my disease of addiction. It is because of those desperate acts of blind faith that I have been given a plethora of friends on whom I can depend—twenty-four hours a day!

Not only can I depend on these people, but I can also trust that God will speak to me through them. There have been many times when I have picked up the phone to reach out to someone and have been greeted with an answering machine. I have been forced to continue calling others in my support group until someone answers. And it is that person who tells me exactly what I need to hear at the time—not always what I want to hear, but what I need to hear. God always finds a way to guide me; very often He uses my friends.

Today: I will remember that I am not alone in this world. No matter what is going on in my life today, there is someone I can call.

February 23

Accepting Imperfection

Cinderella and the prince lived happily ever after. Sleeping Beauty, Snow White, Ariel, and Belle did the same with their own handsome princes. Once the initial roadblock is overcome, the fairytale paints a perfect picture.

The trouble with that ideal is that I believed it. I believed that I would find a knight in shining armor to sweep me off my feet and carry me in his arms for all eternity. I searched for him for a long time.

What an unfair ideal to set upon each guy I took a liking to over the years. And what an unfair ideal to set upon myself. I expected perfection from myself as well. If I was to match up with a prince, then I must be a princess. It was impossible, and several failed relationships lie in my path as proof.

Accepting imperfection—in my mate and in myself—has helped me to appreciate the gift of being part of a couple. We make mistakes. We sometimes say things that we wish we hadn't said. We forget appointments and find ourselves wrapped up in our own worries. But we also laugh together and appreciate each other's strengths. We kiss each other goodnight and share responsibilities around the house. We support each other's dreams and take time to relax together. And we know we aren't perfect, and that's okay.

Today: I will remember that my relationship isn't perfect, and neither is anyone else's.

Facing Myself

February 24

Denying my character defects and limitations has been one of the many ways I have stunted my own personal growth. Pushing aside the things about myself—or better yet, ignoring them by drinking or eating to excess—has allowed my conscience a break from the guilt and shame of recognizing my true self. The manipulative energy it takes to keep up with avoiding my shortcomings is exhausting!

Through recovery, I have learned that facing myself in the mirror every morning is a lot easier if I recognize the true me on a daily basis. If I take the time to talk to God each day and ask for guidance, I find that He shows me how to behave in situations that used to render me insane. If I work at my recovery regularly, I find that I can take responsibility for who I am and the things I've done, and become a more respectable and dignified person. If I make amends to those closest to me by living a better life, I find I can put my head down on the pillow at night and sleep soundly.

There is only one thing that running from myself has ever done for me: it has led me to my addictions. For today, I am not willing to pick up those addictive substances in order to avoid feeling uncomfortable. For today, I will face who I am, no matter what.

Today: I will remember that no matter how I feel about myself today, it is better to feel it and grow from it than to run from it and allow it to slowly destroy me.

February 25

My Friends Are My Mirror

When I first began my recovery from addiction, I often heard people say, "Allow us to love you until you can love yourself." At first I took offense to that. How could they possibly love me? They didn't even know me. As I have recovered, I have recognized that those recovering addicts knew me much better than I knew myself when I first arrived. I despised myself. I considered myself a weak, pathetic loser. They knew I was really just a sick person who needed help to get well.

It has been a blessing for me to meet so many accepting, loving people along my path of recovery. They have allowed me to be me, even on my worst days, and they have loved me anyway. They have told me when I needed to step back and take a look at myself without judging me or speaking to me in a condescending way. They have shared only their experience with me, which in turn has offered me the opportunity to live my life as my own, accepting the experiences that I could relate to and appreciating those which I could not.

My friends in recovery have held up a mirror which has reflected a beauty within that I never even knew existed, and the only reason I could see that vision of myself was because of their unconditional acceptance.

Today: I will remember that when I'm feeling bad about myself, all I need to do to remember the goodness within is talk to a trusted friend.

Turn Up The Radio

February 26

One of my favorite gifts to give to friends is a CD with songs of my choosing. For my friend who is going through a break-up, I create a CD packed with melodies that inspire women to carry on no matter what. (I also include one or two tunes that scream revenge for the fool who broke her heart.) For my friend who has lost his job and is struggling to make ends meet, I create a CD of encouragement mixed with triumph... the songs that got Rocky the heavyweight title and Rudy the chance to play one game of Notre Dame football. And for my friend who is about to walk down the aisle, I create a CD of love songs from movies and television that lift the spirit and embrace God's greatest gift.

My gift to myself as I create these arrangements of ballads and rock 'n' roll compositions is to make a copy of each CD for myself. Listening to music has always been a healthy escape for me. And with each creation for a friend, I also produce for myself a twenty-song escape for the future me—the me who will feel her heart break again, the me who will struggle to overcome obstacles and face fierce challenges, and the me who will rejoice in the deepness of love given and received.

Today: I will remember that when I'm sad, turning on the radio may brighten my mood—or, at the very least, help me to feel less alone.

"It" Matters

To be patient and keep taking one step at a time, relying on faith that I am moving in the right direction, is one of the most difficult things to do. The story of William Wilberforce, the English politician who fought for over twenty-five years to pass a law abolishing slave trade, is a beautiful testament to just that. With each step, he questioned if he was headed in the right direction, truly following God's will. In hindsight, we can clearly see that every day he was alive on this earth was needed to carry out God's will through him. Without the luxury of hindsight, it was only his faith in God that kept him going through illness, doubt, and what often seemed like unending defeat.

As I hear stories about such accomplishments in the lives of others, I am struck by my lack of faith in my own journey. How often do I feel hopeless going to my job for which I have no passion? How many times do I wonder what's the point of it all anyway—my life, my dreams, my talents? Does any of it really matter?

After hearing the story of Mr. Wilberforce, there is one thing I do know: "it" does matter. Whatever "it" is, on any given day it matters. Even if my "it" is to be a part of someone else's larger vision, like Wilberforce's butler, who often quoted Sir Francis Bacon to him during times of bleakness, "it" matters. Whether it is a simple kindness I give to another, or my willingness to work hard even when I don't understand why, "it" matters.

TODAY: I will remember that each step taken in faith will continue my journey (however slow it may seem) on God's path.

Acting And Reacting Peacefully

February 28

I cannot be graceful when yelling at someone. I cannot be dignified if I'm throwing a hissy-fit like a two-year-old who isn't getting her way. I cannot exercise self-respect as I continue to consume the same resentments that have always kept me prisoner to the past.

Acting with grace, dignity, and self-respect are ways of acting in a peaceful manner. Instead of yelling when I'm angry, I can take a deep breath and pray for the words God wants me to use. Instead of throwing a fit when things don't work out my way, I can appreciate the lesson I'm learning from the setback. Instead of regurgitating resentments, I can look within to the source of that bitterness and pray to be more forgiving.

It is a tall order for sure, to act with grace, dignity, and self-respect. Like most others, I want what I want, when I want it. When I don't get it, my first instinct is to stomp my feet and let you know how unfair it all is. But as I continue my daily contact with God, asking for His will to be carried out through me, I am more apt to lean toward that light.

Today: I will remember that as long as I'm living amongst other human beings, there will always be conflict in my life. How I react, or choose not to react, to those conflicts will be the foundation of each relationship I have with another.

Worthy Of Love

I have spent a lot of time in my life looking for love. As a young girl, I fantasized about men on TV and in the movies—they would be my heroes and rescue me. As a teen, I looked to boys in school who I hoped would ask me on a date and give me an identity as their girlfriend. In college and after graduating, I thought getting married would make me happy and content. I wanted love so desperately, but I didn't know what it truly was.

Finding the way to "true" love has been an amazing journey for me. Through failed relationships and several mishaps and disasters in my personal life, I found my way to intense therapy with a certified addictions counselor. By staying clean and following the guidance of that counselor, I discovered that I am worthy of love. In fact, I realized that I actually like who I am.

That realization, along with a stronger relationship with God, has helped me to allow love to enter my life—not just in my marriage, but also with friends and others with whom I may share only a few minutes each day. For me, love is respect, acceptance, and appreciation, all embraced in one moment of time. It can be given and received through words, facial expressions, or a simple sigh. But it isn't something I can go looking for—only something that can be found from looking within.

TODAY: I will remember that each moment in my day is an opportunity to give or receive love. How will I respect, accept, and appreciate myself and others today?

Criticizing Others Doesn't Erase My Mistakes

March 1

Too often, I find myself cutting down the character or personality of someone I work with, a family member, or even a friend. Whether I do it out loud, through gossip or complaining, or silently in my own mind, judging and ridiculing the person's decisions and actions, doesn't matter. However I do it, I am using someone else's short-comings to feel better about myself. My judgment of others is a sign that there is something about me with which I am uncomfortable.

Further, as I sit in judgment and gossip about someone, I become less attractive—not only to those around me, but also to myself. It is time to step back and take into consideration the importance of my own moral code. Is this "gossip session" or "character assassination" worth turning my back on my wish to be a better person? Am I behaving in a self-righteous and condemnatory way? Would I be saying these same things if the person being talked about was present?

As I come to believe that my beauty shines from a foundation within me, I realize that ugly thoughts and feelings need to be relinquished as quickly and as productively as possible. I need to write out my resentments, call a friend, or pray for acceptance instead of pointing my finger and name-calling. I need to look at myself and my own actions before judging the people around me.

Today: I will remember that when I feel critical of others, it is time to check my own behaviors, thoughts, and actions.

Love The Brat

I am the youngest of four children. I am the baby of the family, the brat. My eldest sister is six years older than I. When we were growing up, she always picked me to be on her team when we played touch football. She took me out of the house to the mall or the movies when she started driving. She let me hang out in her room to avoid the craziness that made up our dysfunctional home. She took care of me.

Today, I know I was truly a pain in the ass. I was a whiner. I thought the whole world revolved around me. I thought what I wanted was more important than what anyone else wanted. I was self-centered and self-absorbed to the extreme. And she loved me anyway.

In return for her acceptance of me, I try to be loving and kind to those around me who may be what some would consider a pain in the ass. I give people the benefit of the doubt more often than not, and smile when I would rather tell them to get out of my space. I may fall short in my level of acceptance, but I try to remember what it felt like to be that rebellious and lonely young girl, and how comforting it always was to know my big sister was there for me, no matter what.

TODAY: I will remember that everyone deserves to be taken care of at one time or another. Today may be my day to practice acceptance and love with someone unruly, rather than turning my back on them.

Take Time To Rest

March 3

Many days, I spend my time running from one place to another, trying to accomplish small errands and big projects. I get to work on time. I get up early to meditate and pray in the morning. I prepare healthy breakfasts, lunches, and dinners for myself and my husband. I send emails to friends, make calls, and provide service to others when I can. I feed the cat. I make the bed. I make the coffee. I clean the dishes and counters. Whew!

I recently sat down and wrote out a "time inventory." One thing I recognized was that squeezing in six hours for sleep each night was becoming a challenge. I knew this meant I had to step back and review my daily commitments and chores. Healthy eating is important. Work is important. Maintaining my recovery program is important. That said, rest is important as well. It was time I started to provide enough time in my daily schedule to get a good night's sleep, and slow down throughout the day to recharge my battery.

There is always time to rest; I just need to make sure I don't ignore my need for it by filling my days with busy-ness.

Today: I will remember that closing my eyes and allowing myself to sleep peacefully is something I deserve. I will make a point of getting enough rest today.

MARCH 4

God—As Anyone Chooses To Understand God

Each and every person on this earth is entitled to his or her opinion about the existence—or non-existence—of God. They can shout it from the rooftops, write it in a blog, or sing it in a song. They can preach it to everyone they meet or keep it quietly to themselves. It is their opinion, and it is their choice how, when, and with whom they will share it.

It took me a long time to believe that previous paragraph. I thought everyone needed to believe what I believed. I feared that if I believed something different, especially if it was different from that of someone I admired, that I could be wrong, and therefore a sinner—and sinners burn in Hell, or at least I used to think so.

Today, I know that nobody else's belief or non-belief makes my belief in God right or wrong. In fact, how I react to an opinion about God that is different than mine illustrates exactly how loving my God is. Today, I can accept these differences and not condemn. I can listen without arguing back defensively. I can smile when I want to cry and scream until someone agrees with me. I can show respect where I once only held self-righteous judgment.

TODAY: I will remember that each person I meet has the right to have their own personal God. Who am I to say what is best for someone else?

Today Is The Day

Today is the day I will begin that project I have long pushed aside. Today is the day I will put down the bottle and pick up recovery. Today is the day I will accept myself for who I truly am.

Right now, at this moment, I will look reality in the eye and embrace it. I will call a friend and ask for help. I will get on my knees and pray for mercy and guidance. I will accept the hardships that come and learn from them instead of choosing to play the victim.

It is my choice what I will do with each moment of today.

Today: I will remember that putting off until tomorrow what can be done today only serves to clutter my mind with negativity. Instead, I can tackle one small task with enthusiasm... just for today.

March 6

Growing Young

When I look in the mirror and see only winkles instead of laugh lines, I know something is wrong. It's true that pre-menopause sucks and hair growing in places where I'd rather it not is unpleasant. But accumulating wisdom and gaining self-confidence are worth every wrinkle, stray hair, and hot flash!

I once heard someone say that I should be grateful for growing older—that it's a privilege many don't get to enjoy. While that suggests I can be grateful that I'm not dead, I have also come to see it as this: As I experience many of life's trials, joys, tribulations, and triumphs, I have the capability of opening my heart and mind to new people, new opinions, and new adventures. Where the younger me might have said, "No thank you, I don't like that," the older me says, "Sure, what the heck, I'll try it!" You see, the older me knows that with each sparkle of a new experience, I will learn something. And in learning, I will gain the wisdom and self-confidence to become young again.

Today: I will remember that my age has nothing to do with how young I feel.

Pause

Take a breather.

TODAY: Ahhhhh.

MARCH 8

I May Not Know, But I Do Have Faith

Just when I think I have it all figured out, something comes up and slaps me in the face to remind me that I'll never have it all figured out. How frustrating this can be!

Sometimes I just want to know the answers. I want to know where life is leading me and how I'm going to get there. I chase after black and white solutions in a world of gray. I try to figure out why my path is winding in a certain direction, and end up lost in a scary, overgrown forest once again.

My life experience has proven to me that I rarely end up knowing anything for sure. Everything I thought I knew ends up being something different as I grow and evolve. The beauty I find in it today, as opposed to the frustration I have often felt, is that in the unknown future, whether near or far, I have the opportunity to develop into the kind of person God wants me to be.

TODAY: I will remember that God will guide my footsteps every moment of every day. My only job is to keep walking and have faith in His path, even when I don't have a clue what that is.

A Reason For Pain

March 9

What a blessing it is to feel pain. I never thought I would believe that, but today I know it is true. When I feel pain, whether physical, emotional or spiritual, I know that there is something about the way I am doing things that must change.

The key for me is to recognize the pain, accept it, and then take action to discover where its foundation lies. If I have a headache, is it because my sinuses are stuffed or because I'm stressed from a hard day at work? If my feet are throbbing, is it because I've run too far on my daily workout, or because it is finally time to call the podiatrist about that bunion? If I feel sad is it because the movie I watched reminded me of difficult childhood moments, or because a loved one has died?

Once I have discovered the reason for my pain, I can call a doctor to set an appointment, look to a friend for comfort, or pray to God for guidance. Whatever I end up doing will be the catalyst to feeling better—and that is progress from the days when I would sit with my pain and wish it to go away.

Today: I will remember that pain is a gift.

Laugh And Be Lightened

Not all my memories of my dysfunctional childhood are sad. Thanks to the sense of humor God granted to those who most need it, there was a lot of laughter in our home.

In fact, my favorite memories from childhood are mostly from times when the extended family attended viewings and funerals for loved ones. The sharing about the person who had died always led to unbridled laughter and hilarity. As a child, those funeral parlors and church basements felt safe to me. The laughter lightened the tension that we all lived in on a daily basis.

Today, my husband runs a company that requires him to be professional, serious, and responsible every day. He works hard to provide a safe and comfortable home for us, and to afford us the luxury of several mini-vacations throughout the year. He pays the bills on time and takes care of our taxes and retirement funds. His mind is constantly working for our present and future well-being. Therefore, my favorite sound in the world is listening to my husband laugh. His from-the-bottom-of-the-gut belly laugh fills my heart with a warmth I can hardly explain. That moment when he forgets everything else and simply dwells in the moment of pure release through laughter is one of the things in life for which I am most grateful.

TODAY: I will remember that laughter is the best medicine. I will allow humor to wash my soul.

Love's Gentle Return

It may sound trite, but it is so true. I have found that when I stop thinking about what I'm missing out on, who's not paying enough attention to me, and how nobody really cares about what's going on in my life, my mind and heart become free to give love to others. And the more I am free to do this, the more I find the love coming back in my direction.

What has tripped me up in the past in regards to this idea was thinking that the love I gave had to come back to me from that specific person. I can see now that sometimes it may not come back from the people I expect it to, but it always does come back. I may let someone out in front of me in a traffic jam, and then later in the day someone holds the elevator when they see me approaching from down the hall. I may send a card to a friend, just to let her know I'm thinking of her, and then receive an email from someone I haven't heard from in years because they were thinking of me as well. Or maybe I leave an anonymous "happy thought" note for my secretary, and when I get home that evening, the spring daffodils have opened and are beaming at me as I pull into the driveway.

If I open my eyes to it, I can see love everywhere around me. And as long as I'm willing to continue stepping out of myself to give love to others, I will be graced with its gentle return.

TODAY: I will remember that worrying about what I'm getting—or not getting—from others hinders my ability to give the love with which God has blessed me.

March 12

Pause And Absorb

Sometimes the best thing I can do is keep my mouth shut.

When a friend comes to me with a problem or my husband needs to vent about what happened during his day at work, it may be best for me to just listen.

When I'm sitting in a meeting at work and have a strong opinion about how we should be doing something, I might want to wait until I've had some time to think about it before blurting out my idea. My own egotism to have my thought heard may not appear as enthusiastic to others as it feels to me at the time.

And, when I'm hurt by something a friend or loved one has said or done to me, the best response may be to swallow back my initial anger and take the matter to God in prayer. In times of reflection, I often find that my perception of something said or done to me can be skewed from what really is. Pausing to keep my mouth shut and absorb the feelings gives me the opportunity to act with grace and dignity in the future, rather than react in the present moment with rage and insolence.

Today: I will remember that silence is golden, especially when it allows me the chance to reflect rather than deflect.

When Being Bad Feels Good

There was a time in my life when being bad felt really good. I got a thrill from defying the rules of my parents' household. I felt empowered every time I got my hands on liquor before I turned the legal drinking age. My blood ran warm through my veins as I told lies about someone I hated. The devil has a wicked way of making me feel really good in order to carry out his plan.

As I walk along my path of recovery from addiction and co-dependency, I find that being bad doesn't feel so good anymore. Now that I have no substances to stuff down any potential feelings of guilt, I don't like having to feel them. Furthermore, I know that if I act out on behaviors that go against my moral code, I will suffer the consequences—one of which is feeling bad about the person I am today. Since I no longer need to wallow in the misery of myself to feel special, I find that feeling anything close to that has become abhorrent to me.

It is true that the voice of the devil can be convincing, especially when I am not spiritually fit. So, for today, I choose to talk to God before I do anything else.

TODAY: I will remember that when something that goes against my moral code makes me feel good, I need to check myself and say a prayer.

What If God Is Watching?

Would you cut that guy off in traffic if Mother Teresa were sitting in the back seat of your car? Would you ignore the homeless woman on the street if you were holding hands with Gandhi? Would you make fun of your boss if his wife was having lunch with you and one of your co-workers? Would you cheat on your spouse if Jesus were watching? I'm guessing you would answer "No!" to all of those questions!

How often do we do things that we would never do had someone else been in the room? Yes, we are human beings and human beings make mistakes; there is no doubt about that. But there are times when what we do isn't a mistake, but rather a pre-meditated action. Those are the times when we need to stop and think about what we are about to do or say.

When my head hits the pillow tonight, I want to close my eyes knowing that God has walked with me throughout the day, without disappointment or approval, but with true acceptance and love. How difficult I make that for Him when I treat others poorly or act in a deceitful way.

TODAY: I will remember that whether alone or with others, my words and actions are known.

I Am Enough

When I was a kid, I wanted to be voted captain of the softball team. I wished I was pretty enough to be chosen as Homecoming Queen. I didn't miss a day of high school just so I could get a plaque for perfect attendance. I thought an award, a certificate, a diploma, or a medal would make me feel like I was enough.

I received the award for Most Valuable Player on the girls' field hockey team during my senior year of high school. I've had poems published in my college's literary magazine. I've been given certificates of appreciation from places where I've worked or volunteered. None of those things ever made me feel like I was enough.

My "enough" has been a long process of looking within, facing the horrors of the past, and moving beyond the state of victimhood I created for myself along the way. I have found my "enough" as I stand each day before God and offer myself to Him, to do with me as He wishes. In that, I have faith in His guidance and His path for me—and if that is not enough, nothing ever will be.

TODAY: I will remember that God doesn't make junk. I am enough.

MARCH 16

Grateful, No Matter What

When I first started my journey of recovery from addiction, a wise friend suggested I sit down each day and write out a gratitude list. She said it would be good for me to recognize five things every day for which I was grateful. She also recommended that after each person, item, feeling, or opportunity on my list, I write why I am grateful for it. Her final word to me was that I attempt to choose five different things to put on my list each day.

As I followed the suggestion of my friend, an amazing thing happened to me. The world and the people around me started to turn from a dirty gray to soft shades of yellow, orange, and magenta. I started to notice flowers blooming, birds chirping, smiles on faces, and music that lifted my spirits. And, with each new recognition of the world's beauty, I found myself wanting to do something nice for someone else. I felt an urge to put something good back into the world.

Every day is not a breath-taking sunrise or a melody of chirping birds, but every day is beautiful. The key to seeing that beauty is in sharing my gratitude.

TODAY: I will remember that gratitude can color brightness into even the darkest of days.

A Little Bit More Me

My dysfunctional family of origin, the job I have, the beliefs of my friends, and my spouse's point of view do not define me. As a grown-up, I am no longer a victim of the events of my childhood, nor must I accept the label of teacher or waitress or fork-lift operator. My opinions are my own and are worthy of sharing or keeping to myself, whichever I choose.

Today I have the opportunity to be whoever I want to be. I can pick up a new hobby that I have always wondered about, or take lessons to learn how to play the violin. I can walk outside instead of on the treadmill in the gym, or I can go to a yoga class. I can set boundaries in my relationships so I can know the respect and honesty of my spouse, family, and friends. And if I'm in a relationship that is uncomfortable for me, or abusive in any way, I can walk away.

Some of these behaviors may be new for me. I may feel frightened during moments when I speak my truth or maintain my position on a certain topic. But today, I can walk through the fear and know that I'll be a little bit stronger and a little bit more "me" on the other side of it.

Today: I will remember that I don't have to be anyone other than me.

MARCH 18

It's All Right To Cry

I remember a song from my childhood entitled "It's All Right to Cry." I listened to that song in the confines of my tiny room and wished I could believe it. But when I went out into the world and had an occasion to feel the need to cry, what I heard was: "Big girls don't cry." "Buck up, camper." "You're such a cry-baby."

People in today's society don't like to see someone cry. If a child cries, they are "being a brat." If an adult cries, they are "needy and emotional." Who among us wants to be considered any of those things? I certainly do not. But, I also know that I am worthy of feeling my feelings and moving beyond them. Sometimes a good, hearty cry is the only way to do that.

So, in the safety of my home, or with a trusted friend, a good cry serves to sooth my frustrations and cleanse my soul. And, if need be, I will cry in front of others, whether they like it or not.

TODAY: I will remember that it is all right to cry.

Being Okay With Me

"If only my father had been more supportive, I'd have more self-confidence today." "If you hadn't laughed at me, I would not have felt so bad about how I acted." "I'll know I'm good enough if you tell me you love me."

So often I have muttered comments similar to those listed above. I have thought that those around me had the ability to change my mood or make me feel a certain way. The reality is that, yes, I can feel hurt and sad, and even angry by the comments and behaviors of others, but they don't make me feel that way. How I feel about myself and my own life determines that.

Instead of taking it personally when a friend points out that I'm having a "bad hair day," I can whisper my favorite prayer: "Bless her, change me." For what I have learned is that more often than not, when someone speaks or acts harshly, it has nothing to do with me. That friend may have had a rough start to her day when her car wouldn't start or she got stuck in traffic. Or she may be feeling uncomfortable about one of her own physical characteristics and pointing out a defect about me may make her feel better, if only for a short time, about herself. Furthermore, as long as I'm okay with my hair today, it doesn't matter what someone else thinks. I don't have to run to the bathroom in tears and try to mend my rat's nest of a hairdo. I can respond with a simple, "thanks for sharing."

Today: I will remember that what other people think of me is none of my business. As long as I'm okay with me, I deserve to feel good.

MARCH 20

Springtime Is Nature's Party

Spring! What a beautiful time to be alive!

Go outside. Take time to notice leaves on trees, neighborhood bushes, and the grass as they all turn into their vibrant summer green. Breathe in the fresh scent of flowers that fill the air with their energy. Turn off the TV and radio and wake to the chirping of bird families who have come to visit from the south. Turn your face to the sun and allow its radiance to shine upon you. Take a child to a park and climb the monkey bars. Watch as the mother duck leads her furry, yellow babies across a sparkling lake.

Don't miss out on nature's party.

TODAY: I will remember that springtime only comes once a year.

Each Moment Has Meaning

So often I look at my life and wish things were different. I wish I had a job that I liked more. I wish I didn't have to get to the grocery to pick up milk. I wish I could just beam myself home after a long day, instead of heading to a dinner meeting with my recovery friends. Sometimes it all just seems to get in the way of what I really want to do.

What I've learned is that my job, the trip to the grocery store, and dinner with friends are all just the next thing. Perhaps I'll meet someone at my job who helps me to move along to the next part of my career. Maybe the cashier at the grocery store needs to hear my "thank you" and "have a great night." It could be that my dinner with recovery friends is the medicine I need to feel more grounded and energized in my program. Or maybe nothing that I know of occurs, but my presence in one of those places is needed for some other reason.

I can't possibly know what every moment in my life means, but I can have faith that each moment does have meaning. And with each next thing, no matter how insignificant or tedious it may seem, I am learning and growing into a healthier, more spiritual person.

Today: I will remember that no matter what is next, it is exactly where I am supposed to be.

MARCH 22

Married To A Human

"And they lived happily ever after..."

Ah, how I believed that sentiment with each new fairytale I read as a little girl. The handsome prince would one day arrive to sweep me off my feet, just as he had for Cinderella and Sleeping Beauty. He would rescue me from the horrors of my childhood. He would protect me from the mean people and circumstances of the world. And above all, he would be perfect, knowing my every thought and giving me everything I needed without request.

Many years and disappointing relationships later, that expectancy has ended with reality. I am human. My husband is human. We both make mistakes and say things we wish we hadn't. Sometimes we're not on the same page as far as moods and desires. We argue. Every now and then, we sulk.

For us, the strength of our marriage is in accepting each other where we are today. Whether good or bad, sick or well, spiritually fit or not, we love each other. And it is through God's loving power that we are able to accept and forgive in the moment.

TODAY: I will remember that I am married to a human being who makes mistakes. When I forgive those mistakes without holding a grudge, I strengthen our union.

No Explanation Necessary

March 23

I always thought I had to come up with a very important reason for declining an invitation to dinner or being unavailable to help a friend. I was sure I would be detested if I didn't have a perfect excuse.

As I have worked on improving myself, and experienced true friendship and acceptance from others, I have learned to accept myself for who I really am. When a friend needs my help—to move to a new apartment or talk about a broken relationship—and I am not emotionally available, it doesn't make me bad or weak. In the past, I would make a million excuses and drone on and on about how sad I was that I couldn't help. Or I would show up and be irritable and argumentative.

Today, I can be honest. I don't have to make excuses or convince you how busy my life is. My reply can be as brief as, "I'm sorry I'm not available to help right now."

For I have found it to be true that when I ask another for help, I don't need to know why they can't help, just that they can't. When it comes down to it, it really isn't my business what is going on in someone else's life. When one friend isn't available, all I have to do is pick up the phone to call another. No excuses needed.

Today: I will remember that whether I'm offering up excuses and explanations or listening to them, my time is as valuable as the next person's. Perhaps this is a moment to keep it simple.

March 24

Choose To Be Happy

How do I choose to live my life today? Is it my desire to act lovingly or to hide behind a cold shield of frustration and resentment? Will I accept the people who cross my path today as being exactly where they are supposed to be at this moment, or will I look at them in judgment and turn away from a potential connection with them? Do I choose to smile or do I choose to frown?

Whether I am treated well or treated poorly, it is my choice which response I give today: love or hostility. I can scream and yell at the driver who cuts in front of me on the highway, or I can ignore their rudeness and sing along to the radio. When I stop at the convenience store for coffee before work, I can wish the cashier a nice day or I can avoid eye contact and rush out without even muttering a "thank you."

When given these opportunities, I need to ask myself, "Which behavior will increase my inner peace today?"

Today: I will remember that Abraham Lincoln was absolutely right when he said, "People are just as happy as they make up their minds to be."

There Is No One Way To Faith

The founders of Alcoholics Anonymous were clear that there was no one right way to faith. Some of the first members of the program were even atheists! The idea was that no matter what one's religious belief, their faith could no longer be in their own ideas or solutions. "Going it alone" wasn't working and it was time to look outside of themselves for the answers.

For me, the search for God has always been a frightening undertaking. As a child, I thought He hated me and was punishing me with an abusive father and a fat body. As I grew older and plunged head first into my addictive behaviors, I felt shame and grief every time I even thought about God and my religious upbringing. But as I have spent the last several years recovering from my addictions, my mind and heart have opened to the relationship with God that I have today: a loving acceptance that I trust to guide my every step.

TODAY: I will remember that each person has a right to his or her own beliefs—and I have a right to listen, absorb, and follow the path that feels best for me.

MARCH 26

Wait And The Way Will Be Cleared

Many times my mind becomes muddled with anger, anxiety, indecision, exaggeration, and gluttony. I want release from my resentments and worries, answers to my questions, and praise for my service to others. And I want it all right now. The problem is that if I act on those desires immediately, I am acting before I can see clearly to a rational solution.

When I take a break, call a friend to ask for guidance, or get on my knees and pray, I am allowing my mind time to work through the feelings and frustrations. It is then that I can calmly listen to the suggestions from my friend, or sit in a meditative peace while I wait for God's answer, whatever that may be. As I exercise self-restraint and self-respect, I am clearing the way to behaving sensibly—and that is a good thing.

TODAY: I will remember that I don't have to act immediately, especially when my mind is agitated. I can take a breather and return to the topic in question at another time.

All Of It Makes Me, Me

I used to think that the time in my life when I was so heavily dependent on my addictions was a time for which I would have guilt and shame forever. The things I did or said that hurt people could never be forgiven. The way I treated myself and my body was heinous in the eyes of God. In addition, the fact that I blamed it all on God would guarantee a spot in Hell for me, no matter how much remorse I had or how many amends I made as I walked the path of recovery that followed.

What I have come to accept today is that those times when I gave in to the devil, when he carried my soul in his back pocket and led me down temptation's path, were times that showed me what I didn't want in life. I didn't know it at the time, but I was being given a wonderful gift: the gift of finding enough desperation to turn my face to the light and ask for help. It was then that I was able to walk with God instead of cower before Him as a shriveling mound of fear and disgrace.

Never before did I realize that my sins could actually be forgiven and I could—for the first time ever—hold my head up to the world instead of shying away from each glance directed my way. I pray that my days of wrestling with the devil are over, and I have an enormous faith that no matter where I am, God will always be walking with me.

TODAY: I will remember that I am a whole person because of all my experiences, bad and good.

MARCH 28

Saved By Constructive Criticism

There was a time when nothing made me feel more uncomfortable than when someone pointed out something unattractive about me. Whether it was a hair out of place, or a question about my ethics, I turned within and felt as if the criticism being shared would be the one that finally brought me to my death. It sounds dramatic, but it's true.

Over the years, there have been many times when I have been "put in my place" or "constructively criticized," as I have shared life experiences with friends, co-workers, and family. As I look back on those moments, I recognize the grace of respectful honesty. I may not have been appreciative at the time, but I can now see the love that was revealed when those who truly cared about me shared their insight on my character, conduct or attitude. And while it wasn't easy for me to hear, it probably wasn't easy for them to say.

The reality I have finally accepted is that on my own, I cannot see that which is hindering my progress in life. I am grateful for the gentle reminders from those closest to me that keep me on the path of growth I pursue each day.

TODAY: I will remember to be thankful to those who love me enough to recognize even the most unattractive parts of me.

You Have My Attention

March 29

Have you ever been in an active conversation when you suddenly realize that you haven't heard a word the other person has said—the entire time they have been talking to you, you were thinking about how you were going to respond or judging their opinions?

I have recognized when this is happening to someone else as I talk to them, and I can say firsthand that it doesn't feel good. As their eyes glaze over and their attention wanes, I belittle myself for droning on and on or sounding like a fool. Is that how I want to make someone else feel? If I am thinking up the most intelligent remark or clever comeback, I may miss the human connection that my soul values most.

Today: I will remember that my purpose in conversation is not to be the wittiest or most intellectual—it is simply to be available to my fellow man.

Success In Every Day

When I wake up in the morning, get ready for work, fix breakfast, and head out the door, am I reveling in the joy of my success or simply going through the motions of another day? I know I have to show up to work because if I don't, I'll eventually get fired, lose that monthly paycheck and health benefits, and end up living on the street. It doesn't matter if this is the job I want or not; I don't have a choice.

I do, however, have a choice at how I will view the day ahead. True, the job I have isn't a dream career, or even close to what I want to be doing with my life, but it is a source of security and an example of the responsible person I have become over the years. There are people in my office whose company I enjoy, and I never would have met them if not for working at the same place. I am good at what I do, and, for the most part, respected by my superiors.

Will I ever be doing what I truly want to be doing with my life? I don't know. What matters is that I keep going, enjoying each day as it comes and appreciating the people and gifts in my path along the way.

TODAY: I will remember that waiting for success only postpones it.

Respecting The Real Me

March 31

Self-respect doesn't come easily—especially for anyone who grew up in a dysfunctional home. The messages I received as a child reinforced my warped belief that I would never be good enough—no matter what I did or said, or how thin or pretty I was. After a while, I embraced those messages and became a self-deprecating and self-pitying victim of my circumstances.

Looking back, I realize that as I walked around in that bubble of hurt, I was blocking any chance I might have at fulfilling relationships, inner peace and happiness. I couldn't allow anyone around me close enough to truly know me, because I didn't truly know myself. I never took the time to discover the real me.

Through many hours in a therapist's office and with much direction from spiritual advisors, I have found my way beyond my indigenous dysfunction. I know that I am not defined by my family of origin, the friends I keep, or the size of my body. I am defined by the way I walk through life.

Today: I will remember that I like me.

April 1

Mental Health Day

Take a day off. Watch a marathon of silly TV shows. Sit in the sun and fall asleep while you're reading. Flip through old picture albums for hours. Sit on a bench in the mall and watch people as they hurriedly go about the business of their day. Call a friend to say nothing. Play computer solitaire until your eyes cross. Sit by water and feed ducks. Do none of the above. You deserve it.

Today: I will remember to waste at least fifteen minutes of my day doing something mindless.

Share Gratitude Instead Of Complaints

I want people to walk away from conversations with me feeling better than they did before we met rather than worse. I don't want to complain. And yet, I still do.

Sometimes my gratitude for all the blessings in my life takes a back seat and I complain up a storm! Something occurs and sets me off, or my spiritual fitness is lacking and I allow the complaints of another to jog my unhappiness until I am voicing it for all to hear. I suppose since I am human complaining is inevitable.

My hope is that I am with caring friends when I do this. I would hate to be around acquaintances or people I've just met and have them think complaining is something I often do. You see, I choose to live my life with an "attitude of gratitude," and when I don't feel that way, I don't feel good about me. And if I don't feel good about me, I have nothing to offer to those with whom I come in contact.

Today: I will remember to think through my complaints before I put a voice to them. Perhaps sharing gratitude instead will lift my mood and the mood of those around me.

April 3

Plan The Plan, Not The Outcome

No matter where you live, tomorrow is already happening somewhere in the world—it's one thing you don't have to worry about.

So, now that that's taken care of, what will I worry about today? How about nothing? What if I simply take this day as it comes to me? The possibilities can be endless; the outcome unknown—but exciting, instead of daunting. If I leave my expectations behind and just allow the day to flow over me, with all its people, words, scents and sounds, all its sights, feelings and moments of wonder, I invite the potential to be in good spirits by the time my head hits the pillow this evening.

While organization can help to keep a life free of stress, there is no need to plan out every moment of every day—and of every tomorrow. I can plan to meet a friend at a certain time, but as for the outcome—that's out of my hands.

Today: I will remember that disappointment often stems from expectations, and when I plan an outcome, I am certainly living in expectations instead of the moment.

The Friend Blessing

April 4

My best friend is not a lot like me. She's the oldest in her family; I'm the baby in mine. She always wanted kids; I never even liked babysitting. She is a focused, career-oriented woman; I still don't know what I want to do when I grow up. She doesn't like Shakespeare; I think he was a genius. You would probably never think we'd be able to be friends, but we are.

Something more powerful than both of us brought us to work at the same place many years ago and the rest, as they say, is history. We've laughed and cried together over men and family and love and loss. We've rejoiced at each other's weddings and celebrated new life when her children were born.

Most importantly, we've been there for each other. As I struggled through the early stages of recovery from my addictions, she took my phone calls, listened to me whine about how hard it was, and has accepted each time of change that has consumed my path along the way. When her first pregnancy was lost, even though I had no idea what to say I was there to hold her while she cried. And when her dad died, I bought books on grieving that she could read to her five-year-old son.

It isn't one thing, but many things, that have brought us closer together over the years. It doesn't matter that we don't agree on everything or connect every single day. What matters is that we have each other—whenever we need—to talk, to cry, to laugh our butts off. If nothing else happens today, that is success.

Today: I will remember that every friend I have—whether near or far—is a blessing.

Surrender To God's Grace

I spent more than twenty years searching for the ultimate diet, the best exercise routine, the secret cure to my problem with food. In all that time, I never found a solution to my problem—only temporary answers to physical conditions. Sure, I found my way to losing forty pounds here and sixty pounds there, and that felt good. However, there was something about me that always returned to the food, no matter how great the plan or the feeling of contentment in a thin body.

Inevitably, I gained all the pounds back, plus a few more each time, and sunk back into despair and regret.

It wasn't until I fully surrendered my problem with food to a power greater than myself—whom I choose to call God—that I was able to find peace. It was then that I let go of the control and the need to know all the answers, and became a blank slate, willing to allow someone else to write the plan for my day.

Through the continued surrender of my food issues, I have learned that anything else I need to take to God will be accepted. If He is able to arrest such an obsession, then I know I can also trust Him with all my problems, all my worries, fears, and especially my dreams.

I have already seen it work in my personal relationships, at work, with my family, and with other obsessions and addictions. His grace is available to me whenever I am willing to hand over the steering wheel.

Today: I will remember that when I get on the bus in the morning, I'll take my seat and let God do the driving. He knows much better which roads to take than I do.

Pulling Weeds

April 6

The things about myself that I don't like—from my past, or from today—that I ignore don't go away. Instead, they grow roots and tangle within all other aspects of my life. They tug at the coattails of any grace I may wear today, and they fight against the courage I've been given to face my fears. They don't just interrupt my progress; they stunt it at every opportunity.

To be rid of these things, I must recognize them and call them what they are. I must face them and accept them as part of me. Even if at one point they were survival mechanisms, they are no longer useful today.

Recognizing the "weeds" and getting on my knees to pull them from their roots may be hard work. That work—that effort—is worth every ounce of strength I can muster. It will free me of the grasp of guilt and shame. It will make my foundation available to new sprouts of expression and behavior that I never even knew existed.

Today: I will remember that fear of recognizing the real me deters my growth.

April 7

Denial Leads To Arrogance

For those of us who find recovery from addiction after many years of living in denial, the journey of self-discovery can be intimidating at times. Yes, I want to like myself better and become more likable to others. In order to do that, I need to look within and become aware of everything about myself. In my case, there were some things about myself that weren't so easy to accept once I uncovered them.

Denial, for me, brought about harsh judgment of others, self-righteous indignation, egotistical bragging, close-minded opinions, and a reluctance to try or accept anything new or different from what I believed. Furthermore, I refused to believe that a person could actually be genuinely happy. My arrogance came in the form of inferiority to others better off than I or superiority to those whom I judged to be of a lesser class or stature. There was never any identification or understanding with anyone around me.

My experience has been that the process of self-discovery has brought about self-awareness. And through self-awareness, those unfortunate characteristics listed above were held up in a mirror in front of me. It was my choice what to do with them—stuff them back down inside with food, alcohol, drugs or men; or face them, understand them, and pray for release from them. And it continues to be my choice as I walk the path of recovery each day.

Today: I will remember that unattractive personal characteristics may surface from time to time; what matters isn't that they are there, but what I choose to do with them.

Knowing What Makes You Happy

April 8

I have spent a lot of time in my life doing things that other people enjoyed and pretending they were things I enjoyed, too. I went camping in a tent, spent hours in antique stores and hunting through garage sales, and listened to heavy metal music. I hate bugs and peeing outside. I have absolutely no interest in the beauty of old things. Heavy metal music gives me a headache. I thought I had to like what you liked in order for you to like me.

Today I know this: It's okay for me to have interests that are different than my friends, family and husband. We don't have to do everything together. And I don't have to do anything or go anywhere that doesn't interest me. In fact, it is better for me to refrain from attending the next outdoor camping trip my friends plan than to go and be miserable the entire time. When I am miserable, I have nothing to offer to those around me.

Knowing what makes me happy is a wonderful place to start each and every day of my life. And I've done enough experimenting to know that nothing outside of myself will ever make me happy if I'm not happy with myself.

Today: I will remember that I can decline an invitation without losing a friend.

April 9

Thinking Isn't Doing

I have spent a lot of time in my mind, thinking about what I'm going to do for a living, how I'm going to write the great American novel, produce movies and television shows, and become the most impressive storyteller who ever walked the face of this earth. I even thought about what I'd wear when Oprah had me on her show.

In all that time of thinking through my fantastic future, I never progressed with my writing, and I stayed stuck and unhappy in a job that didn't fulfill even one percent of my vision. It wasn't until I stopped thinking about it and just started doing it that stuff started to happen for me. I started writing, slowly and unsurely, until I found a voice in a genre about which I had never fantasized writing. It just happened. Then, when I took a frightening step and sent off some pieces of the writing to one of my favorite authors, the next pieces began falling into place. Now, a personal daily goal keeps me on track and the thought process is about the writing, not about the fame, the money, or any outcome from the writing.

I'm still working that same unfulfilling job because it continues to serve its purpose of paying the bills. The only difference now is that I don't feel stuck. I feel hopeful that there will be a day, perhaps sooner rather than later, when I can move on from it, to write and read and learn for all the rest of my days.

Today: I will remember that thinking about doing isn't doing, it's just thinking.

Quiet Time

April 10

I need to be at work at 8:00 a.m. By choice, my alarm goes off at 5:00 a.m. After the essential shower for waking up, I spend forty-five beautiful minutes of absolute quiet with myself and with God. I write in my journal, read inspiring works, pray, or meditate. Sometimes my cat will jump on my lap and I'll just listen to her purr as I stroke her soft, fluffy coat. Or, I do nothing.

These forty-five minutes, before I wake my husband and begin the chores of the day, are the most important minutes of my day. Without them, I tend to feel uncomfortable, off-balance, and agitated as my day progresses. This quiet has become the foundation of each day. Thank God.

Today: I will remember that sitting peacefully at the start of my day will aid in my peacefulness throughout the day.

Being Honest With God

When I was a kid, I was taught to kneel down beside my bed, fold my hands together, close my eyes, and bow my head to say my bedtime prayers. In church on Sundays, we knelt at the communion rail and bowed our heads in humility. We repeated prayers and responses placed before us and sang hymns in praise. We learned a routine and stuck to it; the alternative was a hot and sweaty eternity in Hell.

My relationship with God has changed over the years, becoming much more personal and real. I write letters to Him to reveal my deep-down-in-the-gut feelings. When I'm scared or frustrated, I cry out to Him from my car, my bedroom, or the bathroom stall in my office building. When I'm grateful, I go for a walk and thank Him for the beautiful flowers and lively squirrels and bunnies. He knows my heart anyway, so why not share it all with Him honestly, whenever I need to and wherever I am?

I do believe that God would rather I shout out in anger than hold back piously and resent His will in my life. Even when my prayers to Him have been unattractive and irrational, He has still responded with gentle grace and loving guidance. Through the support of close friends, the unexpected note in the mail from a former acquaintance, or the purring of my cat, He showers comfort over me until I can move beyond the anger and continue on once again with faith instead of fear.

TODAY: I will remember that my part in my relationship with God is merely my attitude of honesty—and a true desire to follow His will for me. With that, He can take the reins and guide my every step.

Change Is Reliable

April 12

One thing I can count on is change. No matter what is happening, whether good or bad, it will change.

There was a time when I feared change so much that I subconsciously stalled my life through active addiction to food and alcohol. Those substances melded into my soul and blocked any potential growth or change for the better. I thought I was having fun, doing what I wanted to do for the first time in my life, but what I was really doing was sitting in a thick pile of quicksand. Every time I tried to move, I was pulled farther down into my addictions, closer to death, and miles away from my dreams.

When I surrendered my addictions to God, I was finally able to face my fear of change. Through the guidance of others who had traveled a similar path, I discovered that change doesn't have to be terrifying. It is actually one of the few things in life I can count on to happen—no matter what. It's true that I'd prefer to stay in happy moments when they come, but reality always brings it to a balance with the changes around me. That said, it is comforting to know for certain that when I feel like crap, I can remember that "This too shall pass"—just like everything else does.

Today: I will remember that change is reliable, not threatening.

April 13

Live More, Know Less

I don't know. I absolutely love saying that—and knowing it!

I used to think I had to have all the answers. And if I didn't have the answers, I thought I had to make up something so that you thought I had all the answers. I was so afraid that someone would find out I didn't know something that I would weave together incredible lies until you believed my deception as fact. The problem with making up things all the time is that I had to remember who I told which lie to and when. It was exhausting—and impossible.

Today, I embrace telling you the truth and letting you know that I do not have all the answers. In fact, I have very few of them. As I travel through my life, I feel as though I actually know less than I used to and have become more teachable with each day. I would rather ask questions than know answers. I never thought that would feel like a blessing, but it does.

Today: I will remember to look outside of myself for the answers to my questions.

God's Timetable, Not Mine

April 14

There is so much in this world over which I have absolutely no control. The weather. The health of my loved ones. The crowds at the mall during holiday seasons. The traffic on the way to work each morning. The list goes on and on. So, I ask myself, why do I spend any time worrying about these things?

If the weather interrupts my plans, I can adjust my schedule or sit in self-pity. If a loved one becomes ill, I can give of my time and comfort to them, or be overwhelmed with my own sadness and leave them alone in their suffering. If the crowds at the mall and the traffic on the way to work interfere with my timetable, I can allow myself to become riddled with anxiety, or I can trust that all things will happen perfectly in God's time.

It is so much easier and peaceful to have faith in God's plan; why would I ever give in to worry?

Today: I will remember that God's timetable is just right, even when it seems to complicate my plans.

April 15

What Kindness Can I Share Today?

What can I do today that will make someone else's life a little bit easier, or their day a little brighter? Can I leave a coupon on the shelf in the grocery store next to the product it is for? Can I pay for the fare of the person behind me at the toll both? Can I send an e-card to a friend just to let her know I'm glad she's in my life? Can I take out the garbage even though that's my husband's "job?"

If I have the time and the ability to do all of these things, then why don't I just go ahead and do them? If I'm paying attention to what's going on around me, I will be able to leave "stray gifts" wherever I go. Sometimes I may not get to see the results of my kindness. That won't matter because lightness will fill my heart with each moment that I think of someone other than myself. By the end of my day, I can be filled with so much love that when my head hits the pillow, I will be able to set aside restlessness and enjoy a peaceful night of pleasant dreams.

It sounds trite, I know. Try it. Just for today. Step outside of yourself and spread whatever brightness you know how—no matter how small. See what a difference it will make in your own soul.

Today: I will remember that nothing I do out of kindness is too small.

Resentment Breeds Loneliness

April 16

I sit in misery, feeling the pain of an event over and over again, while the person with whom I'm angry goes about his or her business, possibly having no idea of the hurt I feel. It seems silly when stated that simply, but that's exactly what a grudge is—a.k.a. a resentment.

Walking through life, people often harm each other—sometimes on purpose, but more frequently without any awareness of their insensitivity or selfishness. For me to sit back and take it all in personally is to massage my ego into a monster that will eventually overtake me and leave me terminally unhappy and alone. It is egotistical for me to think that everything everyone says or does in my presence is about me. When someone disagrees with me, it may have nothing to do with what they think of me at all. It may just mean that they don't agree with my opinion. That's not a crime against me. It's every human being's right.

Today: I will remember that I don't have to hold on to every disagreement or provocation with others. I can make sure that my side of the street in the circumstance is clean—and if not, make amends where necessary—and then chalk up the rest to human nature.

April 17

Prayer For God's Will

Dear God:

Please help me to see Your will for me today;
Help me to accept Your will for me today;
And help me to carry out Your will for me today.
Thank you.

Today: I will remember that when I pray this request in the morning, my day is ultimately peaceful and balanced.

Higher Powered

April 18

Is it okay for me to believe something other than what I was taught growing up? Do I need to conform to the beliefs of those closest to me? Will I burn in Hell if I don't believe in God? I have struggled with these questions for many years of my adult life. I have confused the beliefs of the child inside of me with the reality of my faith today. I have lived in despair, as I thought that God kept me alive only to punish me, until I found His grace through my release from my obsession with food and alcohol.

The question that comes to mind today as the most important is this: Where does my belief take me? It doesn't really matter if I believe the story of Christianity that is printed in the New Testament of the Bible—or if I have found my faith on a spiritual path through nature to Mother Earth. What matters is the light that shines on me from that faith, and the light it shows me in the world around me. That light is what will guide me and help me see the world as it really is, rather than how I am. That light will feed me what I need to sprout from my roots and grow.

Today: I will remember that my higher power will guide me, if I have the faith to believe in it.

April 19

Choose Faith

What do I fear? The future? The loss of a loved one? My financial stability? If I have faith in God's plan for me, it is impossible for me to fear any of those things. My faith assures me that no matter what happens, God will never abandon me.

Yet if I sit in fear, agonizing over potential outcomes until my mind aches with all possible calamities, I feed into the dysfunctional relationships of my past, giving them life again—until I wither back into a trembling pile of doubt.

Will I live in faith or fear today? The choice is always mine.

Today: I will remember that each time I step out in faith, I strengthen my relationship with God and develop into more of what He wants for me.

Trying To Fill The Hole In My Soul

April 20

I can be addicted to anything. If some is good then more is better, right?

It's true that addiction is my natural instinct and will control my life if not arrested through a daily commitment to sobriety and honest self-appraisal. The path of recovery from addiction sometimes seems overwhelming, restrictive, and arduous. There were times, especially in early recovery, when I wished there was an easier way.

What I discovered after putting down the food and alcohol and started following the suggestions of those who had gone before me was that I wasn't just addicted to food and alcohol. I was also addicted to shopping, relationships, drama, movies, books, and anything else that would get in the way of me knowing who I really was. As I walked through early recovery, I realized I had to put it all down. In order to truly see myself and make changes to become a better person, I had to stop trying to fill the bottomless pit inside myself with outside influences. It was time to stop grasping for more and start simplifying my life.

The unobtrusive splendor of recovery eventually comforted me as I came face-to-face with all the bad and all the good about myself. Through that honest recognition and self-acceptance, I was finally able to fill the hole in my soul by inviting God into my heart. Only then did the obsession with outside substances truly stop. And only through His grace will the obsession stay stopped.

Today: I will remember that the only thing that can fill the hole inside me is my connection with my God. Anything else is just an illusion.

April 21

Practice Gratitude

When I'm running around from errand to errand and from meeting to meeting, I can quickly become overwhelmed and agitated. I start to wonder when I'll ever find time to spend with friends or just to do what I want to do instead of everything everyone else needs me to do. I wish I didn't have to work full time so that I would have more time each day to take care of the necessities and still have time left over to put up my feet and relax. A full schedule sometimes compels me to put on my self-pity hat.

Instead, I can be grateful that I have such a fulfilling life. I have many friends with whom I enjoy spending time. I am blessed with a job that pays well, offers health benefits, and provides a retirement plan. My interests are many and therefore offer diverse activities that I enjoy. Once I start practicing gratitude, I often forget why I was feeling sorry for myself.

Today: I will remember to be grateful for the many blessings that keep me engaged in life.

Deaf With Denial

APRIL 22

Denial is inflexible. Trying to speak rationally and realistically to a person who is living in denial is like trying to bend a steel girder with only the strength of my hands. It is impossible.

There have been many times when I have tried to help friends and loved ones move beyond their suffering by sharing my own truth—my struggles with addiction, my journey to finding a spiritual grace that has changed the way I see everything, my freedom through surrender. I have found that if my friend or loved one is not ready to hear what I have to say, I can't even begin to break through their walls of rationalization and dismissal. The strength of their denial can only be diminished by a power much greater than I. It is only through that power that a person becomes ready to open his ears and his heart to what is true.

TODAY: I will remember that I am only a vehicle of God's message. How I live my life often speaks much louder to others than what I say to them.

April 23

Take A Break, But Don't Stop

Life is hard work. Maintaining and growing healthy relationships takes a lot of effort. Finding and following the path to my dreams depends on my persistence and perseverance. It can seem so overwhelming sometimes that I find myself being easily persuaded to rest on my laurels, take a break, and pat myself on the back for tirelessly treading life's path.

It is a fact that we all need to take a break from time to time. However, the danger in the break is when it becomes a stop. It is one thing to take a day to relax and unwind, read a good book, or sit in the sun and watch squirrels and bunnies romp about. It's another thing to use the excuse of taking a break to avoid problems in my relationships or give up on a dream because it appears to be so far out of my reach.

So I take the day, and then I get back on track. I call a friend and talk about any fears or confusion I might have. I ask for help from others and I let God guide me back to His path for me.

Today: I will remember that all I have to do to get back on track is get up and start moving. God will take care of the rest.

A True Character

April 24

There was a time in my life when I thought I had to be the life of the party to be liked. I thought I had to be outlandish, crazy, and just a little off my rocker to keep you interested in me. I thought that if you were entertained by me, it meant I was somebody.

What I know today is that what you think of me or how interested you are in me is really none of my business. My character does not come from amusing you or finding a way to be noticed by you. My character is built on moments. One on top of the other—some graceful, others not so graceful—these moments define who I am and show my true character through behaviors, responses, and actions.

Today: I will remember that being a character is fun, but only a surface reaction. My integrity comes from within, and shines only when humbly remembered.

April 25

Agree To Disagree—With Grace

I have spent the majority of my life trying to get other people to believe that I know all the answers. I have discussed and debated, screamed and yelled, and stomped away in anger, feeling frustrated and defeated. I have allowed myself to speak harshly to those I love simply because they didn't agree with my opinion or suggested I was wrong about something.

Today when confronted with opposition, I ask myself, "How important is it, really?" Is my being right worth the possibility of hurting the feelings of a friend, or getting myself black-balled from a committee or club? Do I even need to make an argument for my case, or can I sit back and agree to disagree quietly?

It isn't easy to be silent when I'm passionate about something, and there are times when saying something is appropriate. However, more often than not it is best to zip my lips and nod quietly. It is not my place to right all the wrongs of the world. If I think carefully about my past, I will see that I haven't always been right or had the best ideas about how to go about doing something. What makes me so sure that I'm right today?

Today: I will remember to conjure up my past mistakes in judgment before I go about arguing my present points of interest.

Enjoying The Journey Is Beauty

April 26

I used to spend hours doing my hair, putting on makeup, and making sure everything about my appearance was perfect before I left my house in the morning. I was under the impression that how I looked was more important than anything else in the world. Wasn't it true that the pretty girls all had boyfriends to dance with, while the dorky girls sat alone on the bleachers? I couldn't risk that! Funny thing was that no matter how good I thought I looked, I was the one who ended up asking the guy to dance anyway.

Today, I still spend a lot of time getting ready to leave my house in the morning. In fact, I get up three hours before I need to leave in order to have enough time to make myself presentable. The difference in my routine today is that only about thirty minutes of that time is in front of a mirror. The rest of it is spent in meditation and prayer, and quiet time just for me. During that time, I invite God into my heart and ask for His guidance throughout the day. And each day that I have followed His path, I have been able to feel His beauty glowing inside of me. Whether I'm in sweatpants and a baseball cap, or an evening gown and sparkling jewelry, I am beautiful.

Today: I will remember that the beauty others see in me isn't because of the brand of makeup I apply to my face in the morning; it is because of my passion for the journey through God's grace.

April 27

To Give Respect Is Self-Respect

When I was growing up, my mother taught me to always be respectful of those who were older than I. During wartime, I understood the importance of respecting and appreciating the soldiers who volunteered to protect my country's freedom. In school and in church, I became educated to the fact that teachers and ministers may not have all the answers, but that doesn't mean they don't deserve my respect.

There is a certain amount of humility that comes with showing respect to others. I can't possibly know what it is like to be someone else. Until I have experienced the trials and tribulations of another, I must set aside my judgments and opinions and allow only my admiration for their humanity to show. It is through this state of mind and spirit that I illustrate to others my worthiness of their respect.

Today: I will remember that respect given is self-respect received.

Spread Love, Not Hate

April 28

Like the random act of kindness that spreads throughout the day from one person to another, acts of hatred also travel among the crowd. The only difference seems to be in the rate of movement. While a kind act may slowly move from person to person, it seems that an act of hatred spreads its wings and threatens multitudes with its conceit and loathing. For some reason, it is in our nature to grab hold of our disgust and wring it out onto all those with whom we come in contact. Then, while it "bounces" from person to person, it devours our love and stomps out our tenderness.

Do I have the power to impede the progress of hatred? Absolutely! I can squelch my self-righteous anger by praying for its release. I can refrain from sharing a horror story with a co-worker. I can smile at the person who cuts me off in traffic instead of sharing the well-known hand gesture of poorly treated drivers. I can say the prayer, "bless him, change me," when I am confronted with a person who challenges my serenity. I can choose to act lovingly, even when it hurts.

Today: I will remember that like love, hatred lies within. Which will I choose to nurture today?

April 29

Try Something New

The older I get, the less I know—and because of this, the younger I feel. I don't know why it is, but as I have matured, I have dropped the incessant need to have all the answers. With this new attitude, I have discovered new things and listened to the experiences of others. My interest in something I have never tried before is piqued and before I know it, I am willing to set out on a fresh adventure.

Sometimes it can be scary to step outside of my comfort zone to try something I've never experienced before. The first time I was strapped into a rollercoaster, I was terrified and shaking in my shoes. Had I let that fear hold me back, I never would have discovered how much I enjoy the ups and downs of such an exciting ride. Each new thing presented to me is just like that rollercoaster ride. If I don't try it, I'll never know how much enjoyment I might find in it.

Today: I will remember that trying something new or asking a question about something I don't understand might be just what I need to stay young.

Rough Waters Make Strong Sailors

April 30

Early on in my recovery from my addictions, I experienced something often referred to as "the pink cloud." I was elated with my newfound happiness and freedom. I felt like there was nothing that could ever make me want to use again. I felt empowered and high as a kite.

After a few weeks of gliding along on that pink cloud, I started to come back down to earth. I noticed that my boss expected results at work, whether I woke up on the right side of the recovery bed or not. My family wanted to spend time with me, whether my schedule was open or not. I began to question my actions at every turn. God seemed elusive and judgmental. The seas were definitely not smooth sailing.

Years later, I can see that it was in those more uncertain moments of my recovery journey that I have learned the most. It was then that I stepped outside of myself and asked for more help—from others in recovery and from God. I realized that if I continued to try to fight the battle on my own, I would continue to be lost at sea.

Today: I will remember that when I see rough seas ahead, it is time to look to God and my human support system for help in directing my sails.

I Must Help Myself

For a long time, I prayed and prayed that God would make me thin. Then I would get up off my knees and march directly to the kitchen to look for something to eat. I ate and ate and wondered why God hated me so much that I stayed fat.

When I finally admitted that I had a problem with food, I was able to feel God's strength and comfort in my soul. With each step I took toward strengthening my recovery—making phone calls to others, asking for help, focusing on my own growth instead of judging others, meeting with recovering friends, etc.—my obsession with food was slowly lifted from my shoulders and I was given a new outlook on life.

I can ask God for a healthy, thin body, but He isn't going to come down from Heaven and take the fork out of my hand. I have to be an active participant in my recovery and in my life. His path is always laid out before me. Whether or not I'm willing to follow it is an indicator of how smooth my journey will be.

TODAY: I will remember that my actions to help myself open my heart to God's messages.

Determined and Balanced

Focus and determination are both important factors on the road to success. Whatever God's journey is for me, I will be unable to attain my goals if I do not put my nose to the grindstone and make sacrifices along the way. I also know that balance throughout my life is just as important if I hope to thrive.

When I'm working toward completing a task or finishing a project, I can often lose sight of some other important parts of my life. Am I so focused on my work that I am ignoring my spouse? Do I forget when was the last time I had a leisurely dinner to catch up with a friend? Did I blow off my exercise routine this week because I just couldn't fit it into my schedule? If I answer yes to these questions, I may be in need of a break.

How much fun would a rollercoaster ride be if I knew of every hill, twist, and turn in advance? Isn't it more enjoyable to just hold on tight and enjoy the ride?

Today: I will remember to focus my energy on being determined and balanced. Together they are a winning hand!

Hold On To God

How wonderful it is to have a higher power—a divine being that knows all that will happen to me today and forever—and will never let me walk through any of it alone.

For me, the problem with this is that some days I forget that God is running the show. Some days I pull and gnash and scratch at life, speaking harsh words, glancing sideways at strangers, and worrying about how I'm ever going to have enough money to pay the bills. I behave inappropriately in situations where I should know better and I struggle to figure out my problems on my own.

I suppose these days of self-inflicted separation from God have helped me remember that my effort to connect with Him needs to happen every day—whether life is good or bad. If I keep the lines of communication open daily, I will be more likely to look to Him when I'm overwhelmed, sad, lonely, frustrated, or feeling hopeless.

Today: I will remember that holding steady on to God is my job, not His.

Avoiding Only Prolongs

May 4

I receive an email from a past friend, asking if we can get together for a cup of coffee. I think of all the horrible ways I acted before I found recovery from my addictions. I delete the email and go about my business, thinking that if I ignore my discomfort, it will go away.

A few weeks later, I see that same past friend in line at the post office and I turn and leave the lobby, avoiding any potential contact. As I scurry back to my car, I remember the time I stole twenty bucks from her wallet to buy a case of beer and I cringe. I think to myself, "Whew! That was a close one!"

I spend the next couple of months looking over my shoulder and hoping I won't run into her anywhere. I eventually let my guard down and end up answering my phone without looking at Caller ID. It's her. I'm cornered and I fumble around for an excuse not to see her. My mind is blank and I give in. When we get together, she makes amends to me for her behavior when we were friends. We laugh together as I tell her my fear of seeing her since receiving her email. Gracefully, I am able to make amends to her, as well.

Wouldn't it have been easier for both of us if I had been open to facing my fear and discomfort after receiving that first email?

Today: I will remember that anything I try to avoid will always come back around until I face it.

Resentment Blocks Relationship

There was a time in my life when I got my energy from hating others. My fuel for the day came in the form of judgment, gossip, and hostility. I would never say anything directly to the person who "caused" my wrath, only to anyone around me who would listen. And when no one would listen, I would brood. Thankfully, like a hamster on a wheel, I eventually got tired of running in the same direction and getting nowhere.

After much introspection, I have discovered that when I focus on the imperfections of friends, family, co-workers, and even strangers, I am avoiding facing something about myself. I think there is a part of me that believes that holding on to a resentment and nursing it into an enormous transgression will somehow make me feel better about myself. What inevitably happens is that my anger fills all the corners of my soul and I end up feeling disconnected from God and everyone around me.

Now, instead of allowing rage to energize my soul, I pick up the phone to discuss it with a trusted friend, or I get on my knees and ask God to take it from me. Talking it through always helps me see the reality of every encounter I've had with another—we are all human and will all, at one time or another, hurt each other. More often than not, it isn't personal.

Today: I will remember that if I start my day by filling my spirit with God through prayer and meditation, there will be less room for resentment and anger throughout the day.

Gray Days Happen

May 6

Let's be real. Every now and then, I roll over when the alarm goes off in the morning and curse the fact that I must get out of bed and trudge through another day. As I move through those days, I sometimes wonder why I'm not happy. I remind myself that I'm healthy and married to a wonderful man who is also healthy. I have a job that pays the bills and provides good insurance. I have loads of friends who care about me and my family is not nearly as crazy as they used to be.

So what's my problem? PMS? Is it raining outside? Did I have a nightmare that shook me off balance? Maybe—or maybe not. Nothing specific really has to happen for me to have a bad day. Sometimes it just happens. Sometimes I just feel blue. The good news is the guarantee that no matter what is going on in my life—good or bad—it will change.

The next time I experience a gray day, I can take comfort in the fact that I am human and I will eventually experience a not-so-gray day.

Today: I will remember to express gratitude for the gifts in my life, even if I don't feel like it.

May 7

We Are All Beautiful

Growing up in a family of dysfunction, it was rare that I was ever told I was beautiful, or cute, or pretty. Those words that would be music to any little girl's ears were absent in our home. After a while, the lack of this type of compliment contributed to my already-low self-image. I didn't think there was anything about me that was attractive or desirable, and I tried to fill the hole in my soul with food and alcohol.

As I have recovered from my addictions and walked the path that God has laid before me, I have been introduced to the person that I have always been. Underneath all the shame and self-degradation, there has been an adorable little girl, a charismatic teenager, and a kind and talented woman. She is a good friend and a loving wife. She cares about the people around her and she strives to be a better person with each day. Her heart is open to the will of her higher power.

She is beautiful inside and out—not because people tell her that she is, but because as she works to stay connected to her higher power, she is filled with His grace each day.

Today: I will remember to recognize and verbalize the beauty I see in the children and adults who cross my path.

Love Your Mother

My mother was the product of a dysfunctional family system. Her dad was an active alcoholic throughout his entire life and her mom was a first-class enabler. She spent her entire life knowing that she would never be good enough, pretty enough, smart enough, or talented enough. It's no wonder she picked my father as her dream man—a fifteen-year-old boy who lied to her from the first time they met and rapidly became a raging alcoholic in his late teens and early twenties.

As I was growing up, I never realized how hard my mother worked. A full-time teacher and the mother of four—five, if you count my father—her days sped by non-stop from dawn until the time her head hit the pillow at night. She cooked and cleaned and made sure we ate our vegetables. She read books to us and made each holiday special. She attended every one of our sporting events, school plays, science fairs, and award ceremonies. And on our birthday there was always a party, complete with paper hats, games, cake, and ice cream.

For a long time I blamed my mother for my addictions. She punished or rewarded me with food. She cursed alcohol until it became more appealing than anything else. She pushed me too hard to be a good student. What I know now is that she did the best she could with what she knew. She may not have been the perfect mother, but I always knew this: I was loved, and if I wanted a hug, all I had to do was go to her and I'd be welcomed into her arms. When it comes down to the nitty-gritty, isn't that the most important thing?

TODAY: I will remember that no matter how imperfect she was or may still be today, my mother deserves my respect and love.

One Day At A Time

Looking out into the future and thinking about being stuck in an unfulfilling relationship or job for another year or two or three—or more—can quickly turn my day into a big ball of doom. I become overwhelmed with hopelessness and don't even feel like getting out of bed.

However, when I look at the future with just today in mind, it becomes much easier to face. I can do anything for one day. Tomorrow is another story, but for today, I can handle it—whatever it is.

Some may see this as a way for me to rationalize staying in a place where I am unhappy, but it is really just a way to live in reality without making myself crazy. I can accept that it may be years before the change I want in my life is complete, but I don't have to look there today. All I need to remember is that today is the only day I can do anything about. I can keep moving forward, doing the next right thing in my path, and asking God to guide me. Tomorrow is another day.

Today: I will remember to keep my eyes on the next twenty-four hours only.

Rainbows Will Appear

May 10

One of the most beautiful things I have ever seen was a brilliantly colored rainbow as I drove down the highway. The colors of the rainbow were so bright and dazzling that it took my breath away. I was overwhelmed by its beauty. The effect the rainbow had on me could have also been attributed to the fact that I had just spent over an hour driving at turtle speed through a horrible downpour. During that slow and steady drive, I didn't once think I was going to be rewarded for my patience with the sight of a beautiful rainbow. Instead, I grumbled to myself about what a nuisance the rain was.

My experience with that rainbow and that rainstorm is very similar to my life. As I'm trudging through whatever the next thing is that has to be done throughout my day, I rarely think of the gentle rest I will receive when my head hits the pillow that night. When I'm faced with one of my character defects and know it will take time to work through the ego-shattering that is necessary to be rid of it, I don't think of the peace that will come to me when it is no longer a regular part of who I am.

The rainbow, the rest, the peace. They all emerge eventually.

Today: Instead of grumbling about the next thing, the work, the rain, it might be wise for me to remember that how I travel through the rainy days says a lot about who I am.

Patient With Myself

I prayed this morning to be rid of the desire to gossip. I asked God to take it from me and direct my behavior toward tolerance and acceptance. I felt at peace with my surrender of this defect of character. I drove to work with relief, having turned over such a nasty habit to my higher power.

Within ten minutes of arriving in my office, I was presented with the opportunity to trash the reputation of another employee. I jumped into the conversation and shared my two cents on this person's shortcomings. As soon as I started talking, I felt a tightness forming in my soul. I walked back to my office and cursed myself for acting out again on this ugly behavior. How could I be so mean and thoughtless?

Instead of looking at the negative aspect of this occurrence, I am thankful that as I began to act out on the character defect of gossip, I had a physical reaction that didn't feel good. I can recognize that God was working in me, letting me know that how I was behaving was not okay. Had I not prayed for His help, I might not have had this reaction and would have continued to gossip even more. His grace does work through me, if I give it the opportunity.

TODAY: I will remember to be patient with my own growth. Nobody is able to change in the blink of an eye.

We All Fall Down Sometimes

May 12

Recently I was leaving a restaurant with several friends. There were three steps outside the exit and as I stepped down to the second step, my foot slipped forward and I plopped down onto my backside. While my friends were all concerned that I had been injured because I didn't get up right away, I was simply sitting there laughing at myself.

In the past, I would have been embarrassed, or angry, or even pretended to be injured so no one else would laugh at me. But now it's just funny to me when something like that happens. Instead of taking these missteps in life as a blemish on my character or a sign of imperfection, I look at them as little moments of relief from the daily grind. Each is a moment to giggle and remember that we all fall down sometimes.

Isn't life much easier when we're laughing?

Today: I will remember to laugh at myself and the little flashes of hilarity along life's path.

Stay In Today

When I first stopped drinking, I was overwhelmed by the thought of never having another drink. Wasn't I even going to be able to have a sip of champagne at my own wedding? When I actually asked that question, a new friend asked when I was getting married.

"Oh, I don't know," I replied. "I'm not even dating anyone."

The look on her face was priceless as she then stated, "Well then, I suggest you just worry about getting through today without a drink, and we'll talk about your wedding day when there's actually a groom in the picture."

That all seems so silly now, but back then it was the way I thought about everything. What if this? What if that? How will I ever cope when...?

It all seems so simple now—what do I have to do to get through today with my self-respect intact? That's all there is to it.

Today: I will remember that projecting about future events and outcomes only sets me up for worrying about things I can't control. Instead, I will stay in the moment and think about how I can make today a good one.

My Past Does Not Define Me

May 14

My childhood was difficult. There was a lot of dysfunction. For a long time, I wallowed in the misery and fear that surrounded me while I was growing up. I believed the lies that were presented to me—and the biggest one of all was that I was a mistake. I tried to push the feelings away with food and alcohol, only to find them popping out sideways and hurting everyone near me.

Through hard work and dedication to my program of recovery, I found my way to a counselor who helped me to face the fears of my childhood that for so long I tried to escape. With his guidance and the support of strong and trusted friends, I was able to look my past in the eye, recognize it for what it was, and turn it over to God.

While I have not forgotten the past, I realize that it does not have to define who I am today. It is simply a place where I once was. If the memories rise up, I turn to God for relief. His strength and grace envelop me in love today and remind me that I am not—and never was—a mistake.

Today: I will remember to be grateful for my survival as a child and my thriving as an adult.

Welcoming New Ideas

When I read something that I wrote during my college days, I giggle to myself and thank God for the continued growth He has given me. What a gift it is to continue to evolve as I walk through this life. I can smile as I remember the strong opinions I had as a teenager and the life experiences that helped me open my mind to new ideas along the way.

It isn't always easy to be presented with beliefs that are far beyond my own understanding, but it is always worth the energy it takes me to listen to and attempt to comprehend another point of view. The world suddenly offers a broader spectrum of ideas and I am open to discussion of things that once frightened me. My own thoughts are not insignificant, just different. My views are changing and developing as I become the person God has always wanted me to be.

TODAY: I will remember to welcome differences of opinion, new ideas, and alternative points of view.

Accept, Don't Expect

May 16

Anticipating a surprise. Fantasizing about the perfect wedding day. Assuming that someone will read my mind and know exactly what I need. Oh, how these expectations have broken my heart again and again. As I sit with my demands on others, on events to come, or on the weather, I simply sit in wait of disappointment. I eventually end up resenting that you didn't remember my birthday, that someone showed up late for my wedding, or that it rained on the day of our planned picnic for two.

The reality of life is that I can plan my wedding to be exactly as I want it to be, but I cannot plan the outcome of the actual day. I can hope for a future of romance with the one I love, but I cannot make someone act a certain way. I can look forward to a sunny day in the park, but if it rains that day instead, it is important for me to recognize that the weather is not personally attacking my plans.

It's as simple as this: What will be, will be—whether I expect it or not.

Today: I will remember to discard my expectations so that I can accept others as they are and the world as it is.

May 17

Heroes Are Everywhere

When I was a kid, we had an Italian neighbor who knew I loved spaghetti. Every time he made his special Italian spaghetti sauce, he would pack up a serving and bring it to our home just for me. That may not seem like a heroic act, but it was. I was the youngest of four children in a dysfunctional home. There wasn't a lot of attention to go around, and it wasn't often that I felt noticed. Any time Mr. Messina showed up with that container of spaghetti, I knew I was special.

The only sad thing about this is that I never realized how important Mr. Messina's visits were to me until long after he had died. I never told him how much his thoughtfulness meant to me. Today, I try to pay more attention to the little things people in my life do for me. The thoughtful note from a friend, the extra project a co-worker takes on to help me out, or the email my husband sends just to tell me he loves me—these are heroic acts to me and today I recognize them.

Today: I will remember to thank those around me who help brighten my day. I will also remember that I can be a hero just by doing one small thing to make a difference in someone else's day.

My Chosen Family

When I'm sad, I call a friend and I feel better. When I'm delighted, I call a friend and I feel embraced. When I'm confused, I call a friend and I feel comforted.

My friends are my guides in life, my trusted confidants, and cheerleaders. In going to them, I am never alone or afraid. They carry me when I'm tired and they rejoice with me when I am grateful.

My friends give me the comfort of knowing that I never have to be alone unless I choose to be. How thankful I am for my chosen family.

TODAY: I will call a friend.

Trust God Completely

Part of being human is making mistakes, being selfish, forgetting commitments, etc. Sometimes these unappealing behaviors end up upsetting others or disturbing the peace in our relationships. Most of the time we don't set out to hurt each other; it just happens because of our humanness.

While I don't want to walk around being a distrusting friend, spouse, or co-worker, I do need to remember the fact that all human beings are flawed. When I remember that, it gives me the freedom to withhold my great expectations for perfection from my friends, my spouse, and my co-workers. I can accept each of them for the whole person they are, including the parts of them that may disrupt my mood or interfere with my plans. When I do that, I can love them as I would hope to be loved, flaws and all.

Today: I will put my faith in God, whom I can trust completely.

Surrender Brings Peace

May 20

I don't remember a time in my life when I wasn't fighting against the obsession that ruled my mind more than any other: food. I dieted and exercised until I would collapse into bed at night. I limited my intake of sweets and carbohydrates. I read books about how to get thin and stay thin, and how to recognize the feelings that were bringing me to eat in order to stop using food to push them down. I prayed and prayed that God would make me thin. I thought if I did enough and prayed enough, I would eventually figure out how to eat and think like a normal person.

What I didn't know then was that I have a disease called compulsive overeating. And like all other diseases, I can't fight it or control it by myself. I need others to help me find my way. I need to surrender to the fact that it is a disease. I am not a bad or a weak person because of this. Just like someone with diabetes, I have certain things I need to do on a daily basis to ensure my good health and continued recovery from my disease. Most importantly, the first thing I need to do every day is to surrender to it. With that comes acceptance and the ability to take the next right step on my path of recovery.

Today: I will remember that surrender will bring peace, especially when there is no other choice.

May 21

Understand And Forgive

Can you believe she said that? I'm appalled by the way that man cut in front of me in line! What could be so important that they had to whisper throughout the meeting and disrupt everyone around them?

Sometimes my mind doesn't stop its constant judging questions and observations of those around me. I can find fault with anyone and everyone. In doing so, I allow myself to rise above others and become better—or so I think—because I took the high road.

But what makes me think I am so well-advanced and proper? Do I think I don't make any mistakes or say things that hurt or annoy others? If I do, I'm fooling myself. Just like everyone else, I often speak when it would be better to hold my tongue, or act rudely when I don't even notice I am doing so. Isn't it my hope that when I behave this way, those affected will forgive me and understand that I don't really mean to be hurtful or thoughtless?

Today: I will pray for understanding and forgiveness.

Good Judgment Takes Time And Practice

I have made a lot of poor decisions in my life. I have said some pretty stupid things and I've acted in inappropriate ways. I have left relationships when it would have been better to stay, and I have stayed when it would have been better to leave. On top of all that, I've never been a very good judge of character. I tend to believe what I see and hear in a first meeting with someone before getting to know them, and often end up hurt or betrayed.

From these poor decisions, I have learned that good judgment comes through checking my instincts and motives with a trusted friend or advisor. On my own, I tend to lean toward acting in self-centered ways. Even when I think I'm about to do something good for someone else, my desire is sometimes rooted in selfishness. When I check with someone, I am reminding myself to practice humility and patience in my life. I don't have all the answers, and sometimes it is best for me to wait before jumping into action.

Today: I will remember to take time to pray and meditate, then check my motives with someone else before making decisions.

May 23

How Will I Ever Know If I Don't Ask?

Children ask a lot of questions. Why is the sky blue? Why can't the dog talk? Do statues get cold in the winter? What makes a flower smell so good? Some of these questions may seem simple and even silly to a grown-up, but children ask them anyway—they want to know.

Somewhere along the way, I stopped asking questions. I got the idea in my head that I was supposed to know the answers. When I didn't know something, I told myself not to ask for fear of being "found out" as stupid or inadequate. Instead of asking, I would make things up and pretend I knew the answers to avoid being left behind.

The problem with never asking questions was that I never learned anything new. I felt defeated when I couldn't find the answer on my own, and I eventually stopped looking. I became disinterested in most things and afraid to let anyone see the places inside me that were lacking knowledge or experience.

My pride and ego have always wanted me to remain silent in my confusion. Thankfully, as I have experienced humility through recovery, I have been able to realize that it is okay to not have all the answers. In fact, it feels really good to say, "I don't know, but I can find out!"

Today: I will remember the most important question: If I don't ask, how will I ever know?

Healthy Self-Talk

Like everyone else, I have been offended by others throughout my life. From hurtful words to trusts betrayed and my fanny beaten as punishment, there has been much pain to tolerate along the way. But that pain was, and is, nothing compared to the pain I have inflicted on myself.

The messages I have told and re-told myself over the years have consisted of self-inflicted degradation and shame. I have told myself I will never be good enough. I have called myself stupid for making mistakes. I have refused to accept compliments from others, telling myself they didn't know the real me, and if they did they certainly wouldn't compliment me. I have compared my insides with your outsides and have believed that I am worthless.

Sadly, my diseased mind has a way of taking something that may have been said in an effort to help me and turning it into something shaming. A grade school teacher may have made a suggestion to help me improve my handwriting and my diseased mind convoluted it into a form of humiliation instead of constructive criticism.

However my mind interpreted things in the past is not the issue today. Today, I can look beyond those old messages and discover the truth about myself. My handwriting isn't perfect, and it isn't atrocious either. It just is. Today I can accept my weaknesses without putting myself down. And, more importantly, I can recognize my strengths without allowing my ego to take over. I no longer need to push myself down to feel okay.

Today: I will remember that what I tell myself about who I am is directly connected to how I feel about myself.

May 25

How I View Myself Is How I View The World

There was a time in my life when I saw beauty in nothing. It didn't matter how lovely the flower or how graceful the dancer, I couldn't see beyond what I didn't have. A stunning vase of flowers only magnified the fact that I was without a boyfriend in my life to send me a bouquet. A fairy-like dancer only pointed out that I was overweight and had no one to dance with.

I love the song "What a Wonderful World" by Louis Armstrong. The lyrics speak of nothing but beauty, wonder, growth, and love. I don't know much about Mr. Armstrong's life, but my guess is that even if he experienced struggles and pain along the way, he was in a very peaceful place when he wrote that song. And whatever steps he had to take to find that peace were worth every ounce of energy expended. This I know is true because of my own experience of self-searching and honest, thorough appraisal.

Today I walk by a budding daffodil and my heart swells with appreciation for the magnificence God has given us to color each of our days. Today I watch my niece at her dance recital and applaud her spirit while tears of hope sparkle in my eyes. Today I can see beauty and hope and sparkle and spirit, because I am beautiful and hopeful and have a sparkling spirit.

Today: I will remember to look within when I am finding nothing but negativity around me.

Feed The Inner Angel

It is frightening how quickly my conscience can be quieted by my continued actions against my own morals. The more I gossip, the easier it becomes to degrade the personalities of those around me. The more I point out the negative in others—even if I just think it—the swifter my mind travels to judgment instead of acceptance. The more lies I tell to others and myself, the easier it is to remain in dishonesty and denial.

On the other hand, the more I practice the qualities I wish to radiate, the more they come to me naturally. It can be difficult for me to walk away from a conversation in which someone I dislike is being criticized. My instinct is to stay and share all the horrible things I can think of about that person. But when I walk away from it without saying anything, I am rewarded with inner peace, knowing that I have not contributed to the negativity of that moment. The next time I am confronted with a similar situation, I can remember the peace I felt previously from walking away and walk away again—this time it being a little easier to do so.

Today: I will remember to practice being the person I truly want to be, knowing in my heart that with continued practice that person has a chance to appear.

Freedom Through Surrender

It doesn't matter what my thing is; if I'm addicted to it, it runs my life until I'm willing to surrender my attempts to control it. That's just it in a nutshell. When I surrender to the fact that I'm addicted to food, alcohol, drugs, sex, gambling, or shopping, and I give up trying to have power over it, I am finally free. For the first time in my life, I am free to admit that I have a problem that has me defeated and it is okay to ask someone for help.

My continued freedom from that addiction is directly related to what I do with the suggestions presented to me after I ask for help. Do I follow them without question, remembering that everything I tried to do to control my addiction on my own didn't work? Or, do I squawk at every turn, thinking I can still find a way to use my substance of choice and live a normal life? It's always my choice.

Today: I will remember to surrender my will regarding things over which I have no control.

Be Committed And Flexible

Once I make a decision about something, I tend to take a one-way street to make that something happen. Whether it is taking night classes to finish a degree, planning a party, finding a new job, or getting my hair done in a different style, I make the decision and then I charge off to complete the action.

What I often fail to realize is that just because I have made a decision to do something doesn't mean there is only one way to go about achieving good results. Maybe taking classes on Saturday would fit more conveniently into my schedule. Maybe a luau-themed party isn't the best idea for a friend who doesn't like the beach. Maybe I'll be able to find a new job from letting others know that I'm looking, and not just forwarding my resume out to companies that don't have current openings. And maybe, just maybe, my husband's opinion on how to do my hair may be helpful in choosing the right style.

In all these instances, I don't have to throw any of my ideas out the window, but I can ask for suggestions from those who may be willing to help. I can entertain the option to do something differently than I originally planned without losing my way or changing my decision to act.

Today: I will remember to open my mind to other ways of doing things.

May 29

Hurting Or Helping

In the process of my recovery, I have taken the ever-frightening step to face all the harms that I can remember doing throughout my life. I have made a list of those harms and I have reached out to those people whose names appeared on that list. I have apologized for my wrongdoings and for any hurt I may have caused. I have done this only if I were certain that my presence and remembrance of these things would not cause further harm.

While living in my addiction, I could only see what distressed me. I couldn't look beyond that which interfered with what I wanted, to the lives of those around me. While I sat with family members and friends—some ex, some current—I recognized the enormous consequences that my addiction had on the people close to me. Not only had they spent hours worrying about my well-being, but they were often hurt by things I said and did in an effort to get my next fix. While my intention was never to hurt anyone, my selfish behaviors spoke the opposite.

Today, as I travel through each day, I try to remember that things I say and do will have an effect on the people around me. When I remember that, I have the opportunity to make a living amends to the world by treating everyone with respect.

Today: I will remember that how I act or react in another person's presence may be something they remember for the rest of their lives. Do I want to be remembered as hurting or helping?

The Step In Front Of Me

I hope that one day a publisher will give me the nod of appreciation and set bound pages with my words on a shelf in bookstores across the country. That said, I have no idea if writing will ever put money in my pockets.

What I do know is that I have always achieved inner peace through writing. It is the one thing I can do that feels as if it is coming from a deeper part of me than anything else. At times it is overwhelmingly exhilarating.

These things I know have given me the faith to take the first step. I have committed to myself—and a few trusted friends—that I will write something every day this year. When I first made that commitment, my hope was that at the end of the year, what I have written will be worthy of readers seeking enlightenment. But why I continue to write is due to much more. It is faith in God's plan for me—whatever that may be—and knowing deep down inside that writing has something to do with that.

Today: I will focus on the step in front of me, even if I can't see the entire staircase.

May 31

The Answers Are Within

For most of my life, I have been a black-and-white kind of person. I wanted to know what the answer was and I wanted to be able to regurgitate it back so you would know how smart I was. I couldn't find peace in trying to figure things out on my own; I wanted you to tell me what to do. That way, if things didn't work out, I would have someone to blame.

Becoming true to myself through the gift of recovery from my addictions, I have discovered that no one can tell me how to live my life or what my dreams should be. The life lessons of my friends and family are definitely helpful to me in the process of making my own decisions. Their experiences can be my springboard, if only I open my mind to the possibilities. But what I feel inside will steer me in the direction of my next steps. Only I know what I truly want, need, and enjoy. Only I can answer the questions that block my inner peace.

Today: I will remember that at the end of the day, only I can decide who I become, how I act, and what I do with my life.

Respect All Things

June 1

How difficult it is to have respect and admiration for some of the people and things that I come in contact with each day—the boss who barks orders at me and other staff members, the stranger who cuts in front of me at the convenience store, the Pit Bull who terrorizes all the other dogs in the neighborhood, the snow that piles up in front of my house in need of shoveling and plowing, the obese woman in the grocery store with a cart full of junk food.

I can't even begin to imagine how these people and things add to my day in a positive way. My creator could not have possibly meant for them to be the way they are, even if He did create them, right?

And yet, who am I to question anything on this earth? God's reasoning is not for me to question. God's reasoning is not for me to know. God's will is for me to follow unquestioningly in faith and hope. What His plan is for others and for this world is none of my business, but it is my business to respect and admire His work—all of His work.

Today: I will remember that even if only to show me how I don't want to behave or be, everyone and everything that crosses my path today is a reflection of God's grace.

There's Nothing Attractive About Tooting My Own Horn

When I was in high school I nominated myself for homecoming queen. I thought if other people saw my name on the ballot, they would finally recognize me as pretty, popular, and desirable.

During my college days, I tried to make others recognize how creative I was by being hippy-like, donning tie-dyed shirts, and growing my hair long and stringy. I thought they would appreciate my poetry if they knew I was one who promoted peace and love.

Needless to say, I wasn't voted in as the homecoming queen, and I never did get paid for my poetry. In trying to be what I thought others wanted me to be in order to have a certain status in life, my ego became enormous and overpowered any humility that might have been shown in my creativity and kindness to others.

Today I have a slew of friends because I adore them and they have all helped me to find my way in one sense or another. Today I write because it connects me to my higher power. I don't have to be anything special or act in a certain way to have friends who love me or write poetry that develops my spirituality.

TODAY: I will remember that tooting my own horn—or trying to manipulate others into tooting it—only creates a foul odor on my soul. I'd rather connect with God and my friends peacefully than stink up a room with my arrogance.

The Grace Of God

June 3

"Unless the Lord had given me help, I would soon have dwelt in the silence of death."

Psalms 94:17, New International Version

It doesn't matter what religion you were raised with. It doesn't matter if you believe in God, Buddha, the Great Creator, Mother Earth, or the like. It only matters that you believe in something outside of yourself.

After crying out to God for many years, I finally found my way to the depths of desperation known only by dying men and women. As if I were drowning in a sea of choppy waters, I grasped at the only life preserver I could see. I was willing to put it on and use it exactly as had been instructed, even if I didn't think that to be the best way. I had tried to save myself but my efforts and ideas only had me sinking lower than I ever thought possible.

Had the hand of God not thrown out that life preserver—and opened my eyes to see it—I believe with all my heart that I may not be here today.

Today: I will remember that it is only through the grace of a power greater than myself that I am blessed with life today.

June 4

Taking Care Of Myself

When I first lived on my own and started relying heavily on my addictions, getting to the doctor on an annual basis didn't take priority. When the dentist scolded me for the gingivitis caused by my bingeing on junk food, I was ashamed and didn't go back for over seven years.

As a grownup living in recovery, I was encouraged by others recovering from their addictions to start taking care of myself. I had to re-learn some of the behaviors my mother tried to encourage during my childhood by taking me to the dentist twice a year and to my annual check-up with the pediatrician.

In the beginning of my recovery process, I begrudgingly followed the suggestions by making and showing up for appointments with these healthcare professionals. Today, eight years after a lump was found in my left breast during a routine exam, I am eternally grateful for the willingness to follow suggestion. My doctor sent me to a surgeon, who wasted no time removing the lump, which ended up being benign. What if I had not been seeing the doctor regularly?

Today: I will remember that taking care of myself includes regular visits to the doctor, dentist, and other healthcare professionals as needed.

Cultivate Love

Love in response to hatred, and love will live.
Love in response to indifference, and love will grow.
Love in response to sarcasm, and love will survive.
Love in response to terror, and love will develop.
Love in response to violence, and love will blossom.
Love in response to gossip, and love will intensify.
Love in response to apathy, and love will flourish.
Love in response to scorn, and love will strengthen.
Loving cultivates love.

TODAY: I will remember that love cannot exist without multiplying.

Being Me

For a long time I tried to be what I thought everyone else in the world wanted me to be. I tried to be the best at the sport my older sisters played, because that's what I thought I was supposed to do. I hated the piano, but my mom wanted me to learn how to play it, so I did. I didn't want to go to college, but everyone else in my family went, so I applied and showed up for four years.

When I look back at those days in my life, I see a lot of opportunities I missed because I was so busy being what I thought I was supposed to be. Whether I was trying to be a good student for my parents, or the girl who could drink the most for my party friends, I was always living to please somebody other than myself.

What I do today is for me. My days begin and end with what I need and appreciate most. When I wake up in the morning, I connect with God through prayer and meditation because it fills my soul. I go for a walk at the end of the day because my body needs to feel the energy of nature or show its gratitude for health through movement. I rest with my cat before going to bed. I read a good book. I cherish my friends and family. And I love my husband.

I do all this for me, and in gratitude to God, who has blessed me with this life.

TODAY: I will remember to make sure that I am not transforming myself into something I'm not just to make someone else happy.

God's Will Equals My Happiness

If I find the perfect man to love me, I'll be happy. If I diet down to a size six, I'll be happy. If I get that job I've always wanted, I'll be happy. If I win the lottery, I'll be happy. If only my family wasn't so crazy, I'd be happy!

I have searched for a long time, trying to find happiness in other people, things, places, food, alcohol, drugs—the list goes on and on.

Since I have put down my addictive substances, I have learned how important it is to ask for help, admit that I often don't know what is best for me and others, and trust in God's will. Whew—what a relief!

I never thought I'd be able to be happy without all the things that I perceived as contributing to the perfect life. But today, in a world where addiction runs rampant and people are chained to patterns of behavior that stunt their growth, I feel blessed to have been given the chance to break out of those chains and grow into the person God wants me to be.

TODAY: I will remember that letting go of my will and accepting God's will is how I achieve sustained happiness.

Stand Still And Stay Stuck

As long as I am standing still, I am not moving forward. It's a simple statement and a simple idea, yet often difficult to embrace.

Sometimes I don't want to grow any more. Sometimes the pain of change through honest self-searching feels like too much. Some days I would rather crawl back under the covers and hide than to look within myself for the answers. There are some days when I do just that.

Every once in a while, that's okay, but when one day turns into two, three, and four days it becomes hazardous to my spiritual health and sanity. That is when I begin to feel lethargy set in to my soul and take hold of my gratitude. Hiding under the covers isolates me from my support group and gives me a false sense of comfort.

When this happens, I have two choices: I can stay stuck and risk sliding backwards, or I can face whatever I am most afraid of and embrace another opportunity to evolve.

TODAY: I will remember that when I'm ignoring my need to be truly honest with myself about what needs to be changed about my character, my morals, my behaviors and my life, I am inviting the deterioration of my soul.

We Are All Part Of A Team

Am I a team player? I always thought so. I was a member of several different sports teams while I was growing up and during college. I've never had a desire to play an individual sport like golf or tennis. So I must be a team player, right?

The tougher questions to ask myself are: What am I doing today to contribute to my department at work? When was the last time I volunteered my time to a local charity? Do I even care about the future of the planet on which I live?

To be a team player, I realize I need to care about more than just myself. I need to look outside my own desires and ask what the people and the world around me might need today. Where can I make a difference in the success of my team at work, the community in which I live, and the world?

Today: I will remember to set aside my selfishness and look for ways in which I can contribute to the bigger picture.

Keep On Playing

Terry Bradshaw was one of the greatest quarterbacks to play in the National Football League and yet he still got sacked on several occasions and had to fight through the pain of getting hit. It doesn't matter how good we are at a sport or at life; sometimes we will get hit and it will hurt. The key to overcoming that hit is to get up and keep playing.

What other choice do I have today but to keep on playing? Sure, I could give up on my dream of becoming a writer when I get a rejection letter in the mail. I could push it all aside and just keep working at a job that gives me no fulfillment. But how long will it be before the regret sets in and I start cursing myself a coward?

Today I choose to look the defensive line in the eye and face my fear of getting sacked. It's worth the pain of getting hit, if only to know that I gave it my all.

Today: I will keep playing—no matter how hard I'm hit.

Remember How Far You've Come

One of my greatest hopes is that I can always look back at my life and see how far I've come—in the last three months, the last three years, or the last three decades. There is something essentially beautiful about seeing my own personal growth. It is a satisfaction that can come from no one else's recognition of my progress.

Part of that growth, I pray, is always a sense of humor that opens and expands with each of my foolish words or deeds. In admiring those who have been able to laugh at themselves without demeaning themselves, I have learned to see myself as graceful while clumsy and balanced even when feeling awkward. In my humanness, I am more lovable than I ever was when I was trying to be perfect.

Today: I will remember where I was three years ago and rejoice in the positive ways I have grown.

Walk With Others

When I was turning to my addictive substances to dull the pain of living, I wasn't living—I was being dragged through the living that was going on around me. I was tortured with anything outside of myself. I hated talking to people, going to work, driving anywhere, or seeing my family. I just wanted to be left alone.

Today I find each new day filled with opportunities to walk along with others, living each moment to the best of my abilities and through the grace of God. By putting down my addictive substances and picking up a plan of recovery that works for me, I have found the journey that has always been waiting for me. How much more pleasant the days are now that I don't fight the world.

Today: I will remember to open my heart to the world around me as I walk through life.

There Is Freedom In Acceptance

June 13

Some people believe that human beings are born with addiction. They believe it is a recessive gene that can lie dormant, or raise its ugly head and destroy a life. Other people believe that addiction happens because of upbringing or surroundings during our formative years. For me, it doesn't matter which is true. What matters is that I know I am an addict and I will always be harnessed to my addiction in one way or another.

That said, it is through recovery from my addictions that I have found comfort in its harness. I have learned how to surrender to my powerlessness over my addiction. I have admitted that I don't have the answers and have asked for help. I have followed the direction of those who have gone before me. And I have thanked God every day for offering me this path of recovery. It sounds like a lot to do to become easy within my harness, but it is all worth it—every day.

Today: I will remember that even though my addictions will always be with me, I can still experience freedom if I am willing to do a few simple things each day.

June 14

Peace Is Everywhere

Stop and smell the roses.
Sit quietly outside and breathe in the summer air.
Allow the rays of sunshine to warm your skin.
Walk along the beaches and listen to the waves crashing on the shore.
Follow the trail through the forest to the open meadow.
Take a ride and witness the various colors of autumn leaves.
Jump and play in piles of them.
Smell the change of seasons in the air.
Catch a snowflake on your tongue.
Recognize the splendor of icicles dripping from tree limbs.
Gaze at the blooming daffodils of springtime.
Giggle as the ducklings chase after their mother to the lake.
Stop and thank the heavens.

Today: I will remember to find peace in the natural beauty that surrounds me.

God's Will Is Easier

June 15

Sometimes when I pray, and then go out and live my day, I quickly become the funniest creature I know. I ask God to show me the way. I ask Him to guide my thoughts, actions, and words. I ask Him to give me the courage to face whatever life may bring my way throughout the day. Then, as I go about my day, I entertain gossip sessions with friends and cringe in fear when I am confronted with something outside my level of comfort.

While I want to live my life for God's will, I also want it to be easy. That's where the problem arises. I don't want to have to think about what I'm doing or saying. I don't want to deal with conflicts and confrontations. I want it all to flow by without any ripples or, God forbid, tidal waves!

Over the years, it has become apparent to me that God's will is actually the easier way for me. When I am living the life I believe He wants me to live, the ripples—and even the occasional tidal wave—become almost effortless to overcome. They simply become a part of life instead of a destructive force with which I must wrestle.

Today: I will remember that when I am focusing on God's will for me, I will enjoy—or at least learn from—each moment of every day.

June 16

It's What's Inside

As a person who has been afflicted with an addiction to food, I have never been able to see my physical self as I really am. When I was in a thin body, I thought I looked fat. And when I was morbidly obese, I didn't think I looked that bad. I would look around at other people and think, "At least I'm not as fat as that guy!"

The thing about being addicted to food that's different from other addictions is that those of us who suffer from the compulsion to overeat wear our disease. There's no hiding 100 pounds of extra weight the way you can hide a bottle of alcohol in your sock. When you're morbidly obese, it's not a secret you can keep. The only person you can fool about it is yourself.

To this day, almost twelve years since surrendering to my food addiction and losing and keeping off over 120 pounds, I still don't know what I really look like. I see myself in the mirror every morning and I recognize the thin, healthy me; but by the time I get to work, my mind has converted me back to being a fat girl. This mental transition has slowly improved over the years, and will continue to improve with each day that I refrain from my addiction to food—but it will always be with me.

Today: I will remember to assess my daily recovery on how I feel on the inside, not how I think I might look on the outside.

Pay Attention To The Roadblocks

June 17

When I'm working on a project, looking for a new job, or writing a letter to the editor of the local paper and I come across something that changes my idea of what I wanted to achieve, my first instinct is to stop. I think I must abandon the project, stay in my dead-end job, or stop writing the letter to keep from making a fool of myself. That instinct comes from an old message that tells me that my ideas don't work, so I must be wrong.

What I'm forgetting when I'm listening to that instinct is that I'm not in charge of the path in front of me. Every once in a while, there will be a roadblock on that path to keep me from barreling along toward an end that isn't best for me. I may not understand the reason for it, but I do know that the roadblock is my sign to accept the detour and look for a simpler way of creating something, wait for a better time to look for work, or come up with a more professional approach to sharing my opinion with the public. It doesn't mean I'm wrong or should stop. It simply requires a pause.

Today: I will remember that a roadblock doesn't necessarily mean I should stop. It may just mean I need to open my mind to investigating an alternative path.

June 18

God's Love Is Enough

For a long time I looked to other people to fill my soul with love and comfort. When people didn't fit the bill, I tried finding fulfillment in substances like food, alcohol, and drugs. When those things failed to fill me up, I went shopping, purchased gifts for other people, and threw myself into one project after another—only to continue being disappointed with the results.

I remember once, early on in my recovery from addictions, sitting in a plane about to take off. My boyfriend was sitting beside me but was unwilling to hold my hand during take-off because he found it "silly" for me to be so scared. I closed my eyes and prayed, "God, please help Your love to be enough for me." From that moment on, whenever I have remembered to say that prayer, I have not been disappointed with His results.

Today: I will remember that God's love is as vast and comforting as I need it to be at any given moment.

God's Will, Not Mine

"My Father, if it is possible, may this cup be taken from me. Yet not as I will, but as you will."

Matthew 26:39, New International Version

Even Jesus felt fear and anguish as he anticipated the pain of his upcoming crucifixion. As illustrated in the quote above, he even asked God to take it from him. He didn't want to experience the torture, agony, and suffering that he knew was next on his path.

Why do I beat myself up when I turn my face from the pains and trials along my path? Why do I think myself a bad person for wishing life were easier than it sometimes is? If Jesus was human enough to ask for a pass, why can't I allow myself the same release? Am I not in as much need of comforting and protection as the next person?

Sometimes the path ahead is rocky and uncertain. During those times I may hope for a change in direction, a clearing of debris. Whether that hope is realized or not, the only important thing is that I have faith in God's will for me. Perhaps His will is for me to conquer the rocky path in order to gain strength and wisdom that I would not receive on a smooth road. Would I want to turn from God's will before knowing His plan for me?

TODAY: I will remember that I only need to follow God's path one step at a time. I can do anything for one step that might become overwhelming if I were to view it for a mile.

June 20

Prepare All You Can And Then Accept The Results

I work diligently to update my resume, seek advice from professionals with more experience than I, and prepare thoroughly for the interview process. In return, I am rejected for the one position I think would be best for me. My attitude begins to sour and my enthusiasm for work diminishes greatly. I begin to question everything and complain about my circumstances. Eventually I become depressed and lethargic. Whenever someone asks me how I'm doing, I respond with negativity. I feel lost.

This entire scenario could be different, if only I could remember that what happens next in my life is not up to me. God's plan is not up for debate. My only responsibility is to prepare the best that I can for each next thing and accept the path set before me as it comes—no matter what it is. I can't know what is best for me, especially because I have no way to see into the future. How could I possibly know that if I were offered and accepted the job that I thought was "best for me," I wouldn't have missed out on the opportunity to follow a different career path that I had previously abandoned?

Today: I will remember that God's plan is how my life will be. Finding gratitude, even when that plan doesn't seem right to me, is the best way to improve my attitude about it.

Take A Laugh Vacation

June 21

Have you ever watched a child laugh as a puppy licked his face? At that moment, there is no other thought or care for that child. He is simply enjoying the moment, experiencing love and exuberance. He is on vacation from sharing his toys and being a good boy.

Of course, it's easy for a child to enjoy the moment—he has no bills to pay or work to do. He doesn't have the worries of a grown-up to distract him from fun. He can be carefree.

Today I need to take a pointer from that child. Instead of renting a depressing movie about the end of the world or addicts shooting up, maybe it's time to pick out a good old-fashioned comedy and laugh my butt off. I don't have to be glum unless I choose to be.

Today: I will remember to look for the joy in life—to allow myself to laugh, especially at myself.

Fear And Hate Or Understand And Love

Where does my hatred come from? Did something happen to me as a child that has left a scar deep enough to cloud my mind with thoughts of envy and loathing? Have I opened myself up to harm by trusting or loving or forgiving others too soon? Has my mind been slammed shut by my ignorance of another land, time, or group of people? Must I adhere to this level of hatred in order to feel safe?

If I answer these questions honestly, I find that my fear of something is often at the root of any hate I feel. I may fear a person, institution, or change because I don't understand it or agree with it. My ignorance then works to turn my fear into hatred and I am filled with pain. The other person, place, or thing may not even know of my hatred, or they may be fully aware of it. Either way, my hatred hurts me more than anyone or anything else by cutting me off from any potential for spiritual growth and development.

TODAY: I will remember to recognize when I feel hatred and try to discover the fear that goes with it. Perhaps I can arrive at a place of love or acceptance if I know where my fear comes from.

Comfort Of God

June 23

How often I have felt that God appears to me through the presence of animals. I will be walking along on a hot afternoon and see a doe on the edge of the forest, who quickly bounds off into the trees as her fluffy white tail waves to me. I sit in my dining room with a friend and a hawk lands on the deck outside the window, gazing onto our conversation with recognition and approval. I end a relationship and find myself in the animal shelter, adopting a kitten that spends the next decade-plus bringing joy, love, and companionship to my days.

I can't explain the relationship I've had with my cat, but I do believe with all my heart that she has been a gift from God directly to me. During my darkest moments, her presence in my home was sometimes the only part of the day that kept me from killing myself. During my early days of recovery from addiction and the sometimes harrowing recognition of my character defects, she accepted every part of me without question. She made me laugh with her catnip antics and she warmed my heart with the rhythm of her purr. If that isn't the comfort of God, I don't know what is.

Today: I will remember to spend time with my cat. I may be busy and overwhelmed with life's responsibilities, but I am also her only connection to the world.

June 24

All My Behaviors Affect Others

There was a time when I was able to believe the lie I told myself: that I wasn't hurting anyone when I drank or ate too much; that the only person who may have been hurt by my compulsions was me, and if other people had a problem with that, it was their problem; that my life was mine and nobody else could tell me how to live it.

That lie quickly crumbled as I continued to lash out at those around me when I was unable to get my "food fix" or when I was miserably trying to nurse a hangover. It became painfully clear how much my behavior was hurting others when friends stopped calling and family members didn't want me around. Alone and isolated from everyone I ever cared about, I could no longer ignore the fact that my self-destruction through excessive alcohol and food intake was not only killing my physical body, but it was also harming my relationships and stabbing at the hearts of those who cared about me.

When I put down my drugs of choice and started to live my life for a power greater than myself, I learned how to combat the temptation to pick them back up. Instead of contemplating, I learned to reach out for help. Instead of rationalizing, I learned to think through the compulsive behavior and potential consequences of that behavior. Instead of giving my consent to the craving, I learned how to get on my knees and thank God for another clean day.

Today: I will remember that no matter what sin I contemplate and rationalize, it will hurt others when I give my consent to it.

I Don't Have To Be Grand To Serve God

June 25

I am certain that I will never be an Oscar-winning actress, my body will never be a perfect size four, and I will never live in the White House. None of that is important. What is important today is that I use the skills I have been blessed with to carry God's message to the people around me.

Whether I write the great American novel or a simple editorial piece for a community newsletter doesn't matter at all. What matters is that I do it.

Whether I speak with the charm of the most intelligent and composed lecturers or simply share my own experience, strength, and hope with others doesn't matter at all. What matters is that I do it.

And whether I live a life of grand excitement and impeccable reputation or choose to live quietly and with little recognition for my achievements doesn't matter at all. What matters is that I do it.

Today: I will remember to set aside my need to be better than others and ask only to use my talents and skills to serve God.

June 26

Reasonably Happy

For a very long time, my way of life revolved around grasping at anything available to make me feel good. I thought feeling good all the time would make me feel fulfilled. Unfortunately, with each grasp at the perfect life I grew farther apart from that which would bring me a peace beyond anything I could even imagine: my relationship with God.

As I walk through each day now, praying to accept and carry out God's will, I find that even when things aren't going exactly as I had hoped, I am still reasonably happy. When a fellow employee isn't working up to my standards, I am still at peace. When my husband forgets to ask me how an important meeting went, I still have a grateful heart for our union. When I struggle to make ends meet the week before I receive my monthly paycheck, I can still be available for my friends.

My life does not have to be perfect and I do not have to feel good all the time for me to be reasonably happy.

Today: I will remember that I can be reasonably happy as long as I am willing to be happily reasonable.

Gratitude Helps Me Grow

June 27

One of the best things I ever did for myself was start each day by writing a gratitude list. The exercise was suggested to me by a friend who found my constant complaining to be exhausting. She suggested that I list five things I am grateful for each day, and why I am grateful for them.

At first it was difficult to recognize five different things that I viewed as blessings in my life. I was so accustomed to focusing on the negative that I had a hard time finding joy in anything. But once I committed to completing this list each day, I found myself looking for things to be grateful for. Eventually, I didn't have to look for them at all. Gratitude became a regular part of my day as my mind and heart slowly opened to the world around me.

Where the complaining and negative thinking of my past served only to limit my vision to drabness and self-pitying dissent, the gratitude that flows through my thoughts today is like a bumblebee spreading his pollen over the most colorful flowers I ever could have imagined.

Today: I will remember that sitting in negativity will rot my soul, while living in optimism will fulfill my spirit.

June 28

Not Trying Is Failing

Somewhere along the way, I started to think that if I wasn't going to do something perfectly I might as well not do it at all. With that, I became a great procrastinator, putting things off indefinitely because of the fear inside that told me it would never be good enough.

Where did I get this idea that I have to be perfect? Why do I hold myself to this impossible standard? Some may consider it a defense mechanism. If I don't do something, I can't mess it up. If I keep myself from trying, I cannot fail. The problem is that not trying is failing.

It is my goal each day to reach out to the highest level of creativity I can see and reel in the gifts God has given me to grow in my spirituality and understanding of the world around me. Some days will be smooth sailing, but there are days when I will trip and fall. Those are the days that give me the greatest opportunities—as long as I choose to get up, wipe the dirt from my knees, and keep moving forward.

Today: I will remember that perfection is a brick wall and progress is its bulldozer.

Feel The Feelings

June 29

When I am stuck in my own mind, going round and round about something, I am unable to be present for anyone around me. I need to feel my feelings about whatever is causing my distraction, work through them—with someone else, if necessary—and then let them go. If I don't take the time to recognize what I am feeling, I will never be able to experience peace. Without knowledge and release of my feelings, I become stuck at a certain point on life's path, with no ability to move forward. I must be careful not to rush myself through the feelings, but I must not ignore them either.

In addition to taking care of my own feelings, it is important that I accept my friends and family where they are with their feelings. I must not expect them to ignore what they are feeling just because it will improve my day if they were in a better mood. My relationships will be strengthened when I am patient and understanding.

Today: I will remember that feelings are sometimes the toughest part of the day—for me and for those I care about.

June 30

Open To Suggestion

For a long time I couldn't believe. My life had been so difficult, so tumultuous, and so painful that I couldn't believe God cared about me. In fact, I was certain that God hated me. So when people suggested I pray, I felt lost.

It wasn't until a friend suggested that I "act as if" I had faith. She told me to pray, even if I didn't believe the words that were coming out of my mouth. "How can that work?" I pondered. "Won't God know I'm lying?" Her response was simple: "You don't have anything to lose; you're not talking to Him at all now. At least if you're acting as if, you'll be opening your heart to Him."

I still didn't really "get it," but I was willing to follow my friend's suggestion. Within a short time, I started to feel better, to have more peace throughout my days, to smile without even knowing it. I don't know how it worked, but it did.

Today: I will remember to follow the suggestions of those who I respect, even when I don't believe in them. I never know what waits around the next curve in life and I may miss it if I'm not open to it.

Accept And Encourage

When I look back over my life to see where and when I felt the best about myself, it would be when there were certain people in my life acting as if they liked who I was, exactly as I was.

There was Mr. Messina, our neighbor who thought it was neat that I loved his spaghetti and meatballs, and would make a special batch of it just for me. There was Reverand Segal, who lived across the street and always paid attention to me when I was talking to him. There was Miss Mosellie, the 8th grade language arts teacher who loved my writing and my sense of humor. And there was Mr. Brailo, the high school English teacher whose joy in my being accepted to the college of my choice surpassed even my own.

These people all showed me that I was okay just the way I was. That wasn't a message I received often, and when they bestowed it upon me, it was planted in my heart to grow forever.

Today: I will remember that appreciating others exactly where they are on their path in life is one of the greatest gifts I can give.

July 2

Self-Acceptance And Self-Love

It's a good feeling when others accept me and love me just as I am. It assists in my ability to move forward on my path in life with self-confidence.

More important than acceptance and love from others is when I accept and love myself—exactly where I am at any given moment. I must be able to look at myself in the mirror and know that the person looking back is worthy of my time, my patience, my understanding, and my encouragement. I must find a way to self-acceptance and self-love, or I will eventually wither away and die.

These sound like strong words, and they are. Without self-acceptance there is no acceptance of others. Without acceptance of others there are no real, fulfilling, relationships to be had. Without self-love there is no self-confidence. Without self-confidence I am filled with fear and shy away from many of the opportunities life offers. Without opportunity there is no growth. Without growth, there is no life.

Today: I will remember that appreciating myself exactly where I am on my path in life is one of the greatest gifts I can give to myself.

Find Out By Trying

Sometimes it seems so daunting to set out toward reaching a goal. The end result can be so far away. The work that needs to be completed in order to succeed seems overwhelming. The barriers of fear and self-doubt stand in my path like the imaginary monster that hid in my childhood closet.

I ask myself, "What if I fail?" The more important question to ask is, "How will I know if I never try?"

I have finally come to a place in my life where the fear of not knowing if I can do something is more intense than the fear of failing. Since I spent the majority of my life procrastinating everything out of fear, this is a relatively new awareness for me. I believe this awareness is a gift from my higher power, who I choose to call God. Once I surrendered my life to God, my heart and soul opened to the strength and courage I needed to face whatever needs to be faced at any particular moment.

Today: I will remember that I'd rather fail trying to find out if I can do something than to not try at all.

JULY 4

Right Or Happy?

Recently I was trying to convince someone to believe what I believed. As our conversation progressed, I became so absorbed with swaying this person's opinion that I actually began to feel my chest tightening. I realized that neither of us was willing to admit that we might be wrong, nor could we agree to disagree on the topic at hand. We were at a standstill.

Why is it so important for me to be right? When I am truly honest with myself, I realize that it stems from my desire to be accepted, liked, and respected. When someone disagrees with me, I immediately feel judged and discarded. This feeling has nothing to do with the other person and everything to do with how I feel about myself at that moment. If I am allowing false pride to run through my veins, I feel slighted and rejected. But if I am practicing humility I can admit that I might be wrong, or that there may be a different way to do something. Isn't that a more peaceful way to live?

TODAY: I will remember that my way of doing things isn't the only way, my opinion isn't the only opinion, and my idea isn't always the best way to go. Do I want to be right or do I want to be happy?

Childhood Messages Aren't Always Truth

I remember one moment in my childhood very clearly. It was when my father told me that I was a mistake. I don't remember how old I was at the time; I don't remember what day it was; I don't remember if anyone else was around to hear him say it. All I remember is hearing the words: "You were a mistake."

After a very long process of self-exploration through years of counseling and discovering my spiritual path, I have come to realize that my father's message to me that day had everything to do with what he was feeling about himself and nothing to do with me. I believe God's message is more along the lines of me being a surprise to my parents, rather than a mistake.

Nevertheless, even on my best days I can still experience moments when I feel like I just don't fit in. Whether I'm in a meeting at work or visiting with friends, my distorted thinking sometimes takes me to the place where I'm wondering why I'm included in the conversation. When this happens, I need to take a step back and remember that everyone feels out of place sometimes.

TODAY: I will remember that some of the messages I received when I was a child aren't necessarily real or true. In discussing these messages with friends, I can find my way to discarding the ones that were contaminated with someone else's pain.

July 6

Pray And Take Action

"I pray all the time and nothing happens." "God must not care about me; He never answers my prayers."

These are things I once said or thought constantly. As a child, I was taught to say my bedtime prayers, go to church and Sunday school every week, and trust in God. One thing I never heard anyone say was this: After you pray, you have to get up off your butt and do something. They may have said it, but I never heard it.

I remember when I first admitted my powerlessness over my food addiction. I was whining that I prayed all the time to be thin, but God never stopped me from overeating. A long-timer in my group of recovery friends looked at me and said, "Honey, God's not going to come down out of Heaven and take the fork out of your hand. You gotta do your part and then He'll do the rest."

What a concept! Pray and then take action. In my prayer, I tell God my fears and ask for His help. In my action, I show God my willingness to change by accepting His help.

Today: I will remember to keep moving forward, even when I have no idea what God's plan is for me. As long as I'm in motion and willing to change, He'll show me the way.

Love And Tolerance

Love and tolerance—that is a tall order!

Does my continued growth and sobriety really depend on my adherence to these two things? Must I really tolerate everyone—even the mean people? I'm sure there are conditions and situations where my judgment of others is warranted, right? God can't possibly expect that I will be able to do this. I am only human!

My rationalizing questions will always come between me and God. They will slowly build a wall until one day I turn my back on Him completely and, in turn, fall back into my need for something else to make me feel better about myself. I will pick up a drink or a donut and will be off to the races in my addictions.

My continued growth in recovery absolutely does depend on love and tolerance. While I am not to be a doormat, I must be a person who accepts others—exactly where they are on their path today. I was not born to judge. I was born to live and let others live, and hopefully, in that process help others do the same. How can I do that if I'm not acting with love and tolerance?

TODAY: I will remember that every single person on this earth is a child of God. If I judge someone, I am judging God's handiwork.

July 8

Make Mistakes And Continue To Grow

I have learned more from my mistakes, my poor judgments, my bad behaviors, my moments of rage, and my unfiltered words than I have from any trophy or award I've ever won. Perhaps this is because I need to feel a little bit of pain before I am ready to open my heart and mind to something different than what I have always known. Or maybe it is because I remember the moments when I have made mistakes or said stupid things more clearly than any others.

You see, part of my disease is an image I have of myself as a selfish, self-centered brat. My disease wants me to believe this so I'll feel humiliated and shamed and eventually need to turn to food, alcohol, money, men, etc. in order to feel okay.

The beauty of my higher power is that He has chosen to use this part of me to teach me. Because my memory is so clear on these things, it is easy for God to remind me of them the next time a similar situation presents itself. And because my bad judgment or behavior was painful or uncomfortable, I am able to remember that I didn't like feeling that way, and will be more likely to change.

Today: I will remember that there is no need for me to put myself down or expect I won't make mistakes. Every blunder I make is an opportunity to grow.

Who Needs To Change?

I have a sister who is always late. From the time we were kids, this has driven me crazy. I am an on-time kind of girl. For a long time, I expected my sister to turn into an on-time kind of girl as well. Even though history had shown me over and over again that she was always late, I still expected her to change. I continued to wait for her to go places, making me late also and causing myself unnecessary anxiety.

Today, I have a friend who rarely answers her phone. It is one of her little peccadilloes that she lets calls go to voicemail and only returns those she wants to—and sometimes not right away. When I am in the middle of a crisis, or just need to talk to someone, I don't even consider dialing this friend's number. I enjoy her friendship and she has often helped me to see things from a different perspective, but if I call her when I am in a desperate place, expecting her to answer or get back to me right away, I am having an unrealistic expectation of her.

The lifelong frustration with my sister's tardiness has helped me learn that when a person's behavior is unacceptable to me, I am the one who needs to change. The change may come in the form of me letting go of my guilt and going to an event without someone if they don't show up on time. Or it may come in me taking responsibility for my own needs instead of expecting others to do so.

Today: I will remember that when I have unrealistic expectations of the people around me, they are not at fault—I am.

July 10

Count To Ten And Go To God

"Count to ten before you react." I've received this suggestion from many people who I respect, but it never worked for me. I felt like I was simply counting as quickly as I could so that I could yell and scream and get my way. I wanted what I wanted, when I wanted it, and if you didn't agree with my opinion or my way of doing things, I was going to let you know about it—whether it was immediately, or ten seconds after immediately. Inevitably, I alienated whoever was around me.

Instead of just counting to ten, I need to expand my spirituality every day. I need to start my day by spending time with God. I need to ask for help when I need it and pray for acceptance of others. I need to take the focus of my heart, mind, and soul away from what I want and put it on God's will for me, whatever that may be. Only through His grace will I ever be able to be fair-minded and tolerant of myself and others.

Today: I will remember that if I am quick to share my opinion or manipulate a situation in order to get my own way, I may be isolating myself from someone who needs to hear my message of hope.

We All Strike Out On Occasion

Babe Ruth hit 714 home runs in his career as a baseball player, which lasted over twenty years. That's approximately thirty-five home runs per year. Each major league team played approximately 150 games per year in those days. That means that one of the greatest players in baseball history averaged only one home run per four games he played. How many times do you suppose he struck out? Does it even matter?

TODAY: I will remember that when I allow fear to keep me from trying something, I am taking an action that may keep me from becoming the person I am meant to be. Is that what I want people to remember about me?

July 12

Stop Complaining And Explaining

There was a time in my life when all I would do was complain. I could only seem to conjure up negatives. Once you started complaining with me, I was off and running, lost in a world of endless drama and disappointment.

During this time of my life, I also thought if I said no to a request from someone, I had to go into a long explanation of why I was saying no. I had to convince that person that I truly was unavailable or that my saying no had nothing to do with whether or not I liked them.

Over the years I found that complaining and explaining are exhausting behaviors. I got tired of hearing myself grumble and whine about this and that, and I became weary from making excuses all the time.

What energizes my soul today is appreciating the life that has been given to me and taking care of that life as best as I am able. Sometimes that means I might disappoint someone because I can't be what they want me to be. And sometimes that means accepting my own disappointments without holding anyone else—or God—responsible.

Today: I will remember that no matter what is going on in my life, there is always something to be grateful for. I also know that saying "no" is enough.

Selfishness Equals Atheism

Franklin D. Roosevelt once said that "selfishness is the only real atheism." Atheism is a harsh word to make synonymous with selfishness. Maybe childish would be more appropriate, or even bull-headed—but atheism?

If I am honest with myself, I must admit that when I am sitting in selfishness, I am thinking only of myself. I am not willing to open my mind to the experience of another. I do not think to ask for help because I believe I have all the answers. I can see nothing beyond what I want. I am blocked from all relationships, including my relationship with God.

It is disturbing to think that every time I act selfishly, I am experiencing atheism, but to a certain extent, it is reality. If I am committed to my relationship with God, my selfish desires don't even come to mind. I am nestled safely in His arms, and aspire to be only what He wants me to be.

Today: I will remember to guard myself from selfishness by staying connected to God throughout each moment of the day.

Addicted To Misery

At times, I have been completely addicted to my own suffering. Embracing my role as the victim of childhood abuse, family dysfunction, and mean-spirited bosses, I was able to rock myself to sleep each night with the horror of it all. If you tried to help me out of it too many times, I cut you out of my life.

Overcoming the addiction of that despair was more difficult than it was to admit my powerlessness over alcohol and food. If I wasn't a victim, what was I? If my sour mood wasn't everyone else's fault, who could I blame but myself? It was terrifying to think that I may have held onto my misery on purpose.

Unintentionally, I have clung to unhealthy behaviors and attitudes simply because they were familiar to me. Once the realization set in that these behaviors and attitudes were hurting me and blocking me from spiritual growth, I was able to take action and ask for help in changing.

Today: I will remember that when I feel good from feeling bad, my spiritual life is in danger and it is time to ask for help.

Never All, Never Nothing

Someone once told me that I had an inferiority complex that was masked by a superiority complex. In other words, internally I knew that I would never be enough, while externally I appeared to think I had it all together and was much more important than everyone around me. This was an exhausting way to go through life!

What has become clear to me since putting down the addictive substances that ruled my life for so long is that there will be times when I feel inferior. And there will be other times when I feel superior. But the times when I will feel most balanced and most blessed will be when I can identify similarities with another human being. When I feel understood and can, in turn, understand another, I can have peace.

TODAY: I will remember to look for similarities with others instead of evaluating our differences.

JULY 16

Believing In Myself

I have spent the majority of my life looking for approval. As a child, I wanted approval from my parents, older siblings, and teachers. I wanted them to tell me I was good enough, smart enough, and fun enough. I wanted to be told that I was appreciated.

When those around me failed to tell me what I thought I needed to hear in order to feel good about myself, I swayed in the direction of believing their silence was disapproval. If someone failed to offer praise for something I had done, I thought I had failed. Furthermore, if someone disagreed with me, I believed I was wrong.

Over time, I have learned that the only person whose opinion about me makes any difference in my life is my own. If I don't believe in myself, I am petrified in time and space. If I trust myself and my instincts, I can do anything.

TODAY: I will remember that what other people think of me is none of my business.

Only Love

When I was a teenager, I spent the majority of my waking hours looking for and dreaming about what I thought love was. I imagined an attractive young boy would suddenly look my way and fall head-over-heels in love with me. He would have no choice but to overlook my shyness and tomboy appearance because his heart would swell in my presence. We would live happily ever after.

With maturity comes the knowledge that love is much more than a silly girlhood crush. It is more than a mother's embrace or a father's protection. It is more than a lifelong friendship. And it is more than two people walking down the aisle of a church together. Love is the ultimate journey that mixes faith and trust with willingness and open-mindedness. It holds the soul in arms stronger and gentler than any human being can imagine. Love guides. Love shelters. Love accepts.

Drawn to love first through desire to connect with other human beings, I praise love today for its never-ending patience.

Today: I will remember that I can find love in all the world around me, for it was all designed and created by the one who holds its true meaning.

July 18

What Blocks Me From Love?

When it's the middle of winter and my windshield is icy and covered with snow, it would be downright impossible to see the road without scraping the stubborn pieces of ice from the glass, using the car's defroster to warm the surface, and occasionally engaging the windshield wipers to clear away frozen remnants and new flakes of snow.

My soul, like a car's windshield in the middle of winter, needs to be cleared before love can be felt. The anger and resentments that have accumulated in my gut like garbage in a landfill need to be faced, confronted, and discarded. The prejudices and judgments that have long kept me from appreciating others need to be replaced with acceptance and tolerance. The fear that consistently tells me lies about myself and those around me needs to be overcome with courageous action and trust.

It isn't easy work to become aware of that which is blocking me from love. It is even harder to accept it and battle beyond it. But it is worth every ounce of energy it takes.

Today: I will remember to look my anger, my judgments, my resentments, and my fears right in the eye today. I will not allow these things to keep my soul away from love for one more moment.

Detaching With Love

July 19

If I allow the feelings of another to influence my own mood, I will never achieve pure serenity. While it is human to be affected by those closest to me, I must remember that just because someone I love is sitting in self-pity does not mean I need to take a seat next to them.

I can be supportive of my loved ones without taking responsibility for their moods, or taking on their feelings of resentment, anger, and self-deprecation. Whenever I accept someone exactly where he or she is at a single moment in time, I am acting lovingly. But just because I am accepting them does not mean I am condoning their behavior or enabling their feelings. Once I recognize and accept where they are, I can move on by continuing to carry out my next steps, without the burden of carrying another's pain.

Sometimes it feels a little selfish to go about my business when a friend or loved one is hurting, but I know that if I climb down into the hole of hurt with them, I won't be available to throw them a rope of hope when they are ready to climb out.

Today: I will remember to be empathetic, rather than enabling, with friends and loved ones by remembering that we are all at different places on our journeys.

JULY 20

Accept The Way Things Are

Sometimes I fool myself into believing that life would be easier if I had more money, an easier job, a different group of friends, or fewer responsibilities. I walk around in a cloud of self-pity, wishing that everyone would either agree with me all the time, get out of my way, or just leave me alone.

When I'm stuck in this type of mood, it reminds me of my life before I found my way to a healthy relationship with God. I always felt like it was me against the world. I didn't trust or count on anyone, and everything was always everyone else's fault. It was a lonely way to live.

Today when I find myself sliding backward into this type of thinking, it serves as a sign to check myself and my willingness to continue working toward spiritual growth each day. Nine times out of ten, I find that I've let something slip that helps me to stay balanced. Adjusting that part of my recovery plan is all it will take to start feeling better.

TODAY: I will remember that acceptance is the answer to all my problems, and if I'm having trouble accepting, I know I need to look within myself to find the source of that trouble.

Don't Just Know, Act

July 21

I spent the first twenty-nine years of my life researching how to have a thin, healthy body. I read books about calorie-counting and emotional eating. I joined commercial weight loss groups and attended meetings where I listened to lecture after lecture about how to lose weight and keep it off. I created food plans and exercise routines that would help to keep me svelte. I knew just about everything there was to know about getting and staying thin.

Still, on my twenty-ninth birthday, I was 5'4" and weighed over 250 pounds. It was clear that the amount of knowledge I had acquired did nothing to make me healthy.

Until I admitted I had a reaction to food that was different than normal people—once I started eating, I could not stop, and I could not stop myself from starting—I couldn't grow beyond simple knowledge to true acceptance, which allowed me to take action to change. I had to set aside everything I thought I knew about dieting, exercising, and healthy living, and ask for help. It was time to follow the direction of people with my same problem who had found the solution.

The actions I took then (and still take today) were the keys to my freedom from the twenty-nine years of bondage to compulsive eating and compulsive food behaviors.

Today: I will remember that it doesn't matter how much I think I know about something. Taking action is the only way I can begin to change and grow.

July 22

Acceptance Brings Serenity

When I am accepting of what's going on around me, even if I don't agree with it, I am more at peace. With acceptance of something or someone, I have no expectation that the thing or person will be different. If I am without expectation, I can't be disappointed. When I have no disappointment, I can feel good, balanced, and serene.

For example, if I can accept that my boss is a person who, for whatever reason, can't give a compliment, then I will never expect one—and therefore never be disappointed when he doesn't recognize my hard work. Sure, I'd like to work for someone who appreciates my skills and talents. But I can't change the way someone is, and if I don't accept others as they are, and in turn expect them to change in order to make my life easier, I will inevitably be discouraged.

I don't know how it works or why it works; I just know that acceptance of the world as it is brings serenity to my heart.

Today: I will remember to pray for acceptance. Alone, I lean toward judgment and close-mindedness; with God's help, I can find balance and tolerance.

Filling The Empty Soul

Part of being an addict is wanting to feel better—not tomorrow, not in an hour—right now! That's why drugs, alcohol, food, gambling—anything outside of myself—would work. Because when I'm reaching outside of myself for something else to fill me up, it is tangible. I take a shot of whiskey, eat a pizza, make a bet, have sex with a stranger, etc., and for that moment I forget my pain, my sadness, my emptiness, my anger, or whatever it is I'm trying to escape.

The problem with immediate gratification is that it doesn't stick around for very long. Soon my buzz wears off, I'm hungry again, I lose the bet, or wake up next to the person I don't remember going home with, and my self-disgust is doubled. Now, instead of just feeling whatever I was feeling, I'm also ashamed of myself. The consequence of my immediate gratification has turned into one more thing to feel bad about.

TODAY: I will remember to focus attention on filling my soul with my relationship with God. It may take longer and require more energy than running out to buy a case of beer, but the payoff is fulfillment beyond my wildest dreams.

JULY 24

Staying Sober Is Not Enough

Do nothing except put down the addictive substance. Don't ever pick it up again as long as you live. If you do this I guarantee that you—and everyone around you—will end up being just as miserable as when you were using.

My experience has shown me that once I put down the addictive substance, I had to pick up a higher power, and many other tools for living a sane and happy life. I had to learn how to live through working with others who had also once been addicted. I had to ask for help, pray a lot, and spend time with people who shared my addiction.

For me, the food and alcohol that had me chained to a life of self-degradation were only a side effect to what was really going on inside. I was suffering from a spiritual sickness—a disease that kept me from living the life God had always wanted me to live. Until I was able to recognize that through clean living and surrendering my misguided will, just being sober would never have been enough.

TODAY: I will remember that the path of recovery is lined with many things that will help me to find my way—and only one of those things is refraining from my drug of choice.

Be Patient And Ask For Help

I recently experienced surgery on my foot and now have to sit—literally—through a six-to-eight-week recovery. Even though my doctor has been very clear with me that my foot will not heal if I don't follow his directions and stay off of it, I still feel like I'm ready to go out and run a marathon.

I want to be able to do things for myself. I want to be able to get in the car and drive to the store when I need something. I want to be able to walk down my basement stairs in order to do the laundry. I want to call a friend and meet up for a Saturday afternoon hike.

What I don't want—more than anything listed above that I want—is for my recovery process to take longer than six to eight weeks. Therefore, I need to practice patience. I need to ask others for help, and I need to ask God to grant me enough humility to realize that I am not the only one who knows how to fold the laundry or do the food shopping.

TODAY: I will remember that patience is not just about "idling your motor." It is also about accepting a situation for what it is, following directions of those who know more than I do, and setting my ego aside in order to ask for help.

Everything Changes

Being happy isn't something that I have been accustomed to for my entire life. I have had moments of fleeting laughter, or benign fantasies that clouded out sadness, but true happiness was never something I really knew before I found recovery from addiction.

Then, in the early days of recovery, I was swept up onto the "pink cloud" of relief, thinking I could never feel sad again; I had been freed from the bondage of my addictions and life was wonderful. Before long, that pink cloud burst into a hailstorm of feelings that were, at times, overwhelming. I had no idea how much I was capable of feeling, and to be honest, I wasn't sure I wanted to know!

Fortunately, I was willing to talk about what I was feeling and ask for help from those who had gone before me. They walked me through the difficult times and reminded me that "whether it is good or bad, it will change." I came to realize that the feeling of the moment wasn't forever. If I was sad, happiness would come again; if I was happy, it would also pass, until I found it another day. I just needed to accept each moment for what it was, instead of fearing it might never change.

Today: I will remember that happiness is always within my reach—maybe not to be found and felt today, but most definitely a future state of being.

Change Myself, Not Others

July 27

I can't make my co-workers care more about their jobs. I can't make my husband more affectionate. I can't make my friends more thoughtful and understanding. And I certainly can't make a stranger treat me with respect. Fortunately for me, there is one person I can change: myself.

I can keep my eyes on my own responsibilities at work and stop worrying about what everyone else is or is not doing. I can love my husband exactly the way he is, offering affection to him as I feel it and expecting nothing in return. I can call my friends and ask how they are on a regular basis, and then really listen to them. And I can be respectful to each and every person I meet, no matter how they treat me.

If I am willing to embrace these changes in how I behave with and around others, I will be amazed before just a week goes by.

Today: I will remember that the only person I have any control of changing is myself.

Grow Through Fear

When I was in high school, I was terrified of public speaking. I would lie awake in bed the night before I had to give a speech in one of my classes and think of everything that could go wrong. I could feel my heart beating out of my chest as I walked to the front of the room when my name was called, and I could feel my face flush with embarrassment as soon as I was standing before my peers. I was petrified.

Throughout my high school years, and on through college, it was often a requirement that I give a speech or present an opinion in front of others. I don't remember when it happened, but at some point, I stopped being afraid to stand up and speak. After being forced to do it for so long, I suppose it slowly became something I just accepted as part of the class.

Looking back on this experience, I realize I can apply this solution to whatever I am afraid of today. Being honest about my feelings. Asking for what I need. Confronting a friend with a truth that may be difficult for them to hear. Standing my ground with an over-bearing boss. These are things that I might be able to accept as just another part of life, if I'm willing to face my fears about them today.

Today: I will remember that when I feel fear, it is really an opportunity to face life and grow.

Feel The Sadness And Then Let It Pass

Sometimes I feel sad. I don't like feeling sad, but sometimes I just do. I can tell myself how much better my life is than that of someone who is crippled or blind, or alone and wishing for a loving marriage, but I still feel sad. While I know in my head that I have every reason to be happy—a healthy body, a strong marriage with the man I love, a job that pays me enough to live comfortably, family and friends who care about me—that knowledge can't find a path to my heart.

It's okay. For the time of sadness, I can just feel sad. Maybe I need to feel sad for some reason that I don't understand at the moment. I don't need to try to make it go away. Like everything else in this world, I know that my feeling sad will not be forever. It will pass, as it has before, and I will feel happy again.

TODAY: I will remember that trying to talk myself out of a feeling is like trying to recall the color of the doctor's eyes who delivered me.

JULY 30

Being Okay With Me

Life is so difficult when the only voice I can hear is the one inside my head telling me that nothing I do or say is ever good enough. That voice of low self-esteem had plagued my existence for many years before I was able to open my mind and my heart to a new message.

Growing up in a dysfunctional home didn't often provide for self-esteem building moments. By the time I left home for college, I was already so in hate with myself that the only way to find escape was to drink or eat myself into oblivion.

Only through recovery from my addictions, many years of clean living, and therapeutic diligence, was I able to hear a new voice in my mind. The new voice spoke of forgiveness, hope and love. It allowed me to let go of the constant need to judge myself and hold myself up to impossible standards. It gave me the freedom to be okay with me—just for today.

TODAY: I will remember that every day I need to remind myself that I am a worthy, loveable, and special human being.

Real Friends Bring Honesty

Being famous was something I always wanted for myself. I wanted to be recognized wherever I went. I wanted people to tell me how much they loved me. I wanted to be put on a pedestal and admired.

I realize now that the reason I was so desperate for this type of fame was because I was desperate to be accepted. I thought I needed acclamation and praise from others to be okay.

I know today that what I really need from others is honesty. I need my friends and family to be loving, but also to care about me enough to tell me the truth about what they see in me. If I am being selfish and I cannot see it, I would rather have a friend tell me that is what they see, than to pretend I am being selfless and thoughtful. I will never be able to grow beyond my character limitations if I am surrounded by "yes men."

TODAY: I will remember to open my mind and heart to truth, no matter how much it may hurt.

AUGUST 1

Happiness Is God In My Heart

I used to think happy people were frauds. I knew they were hiding something. I truly did not believe that a person could be happy living in this world. All I saw was misery, loss, abuse, sadness, war, betrayal, gossip, and loneliness. It was all I saw because it was all that was inside of me.

Today, I have power over my attitude and that power lies in my relationship with God. Each morning when I talk to Him, I thank Him for my health, the love in my life, and the beautiful world around me. It is what I see when I look around today, because it is what is inside of me.

It took an awful lot of time and energy to replace my old insides with this new, more peaceful way of looking at life, but it was worth every minute of my time and every ounce of my energy!

TODAY: I will remember that my happiness will remain as long as I am willing to walk with, converse with, and live with God in my heart—one day at a time.

Only God Is Perfect

August 2

When dealing with humans, there is no such thing as perfect. As long as I think I need to be perfect, that is how long I will be frustrated and disappointed. As long as I think life should be perfect, that is how long I will be confused and lost. As long as I think other people should be perfect, that is how long I will be waiting and lonely.

The only perfect that exists is God. Once I am willing to accept this fact, I am free to truly be. Because then, I hear no voice telling me not to do something because I won't be able to do it perfectly. I only feel the guidance of God as I take each step on my journey, messy as it may sometimes be.

Today: I will remember that expecting perfection, from myself and others, is opposing the natural order of God's world.

Don't Preach, Act

Once I found recovery from my addictions, I wanted to shout it from the rooftops of the world! I wanted to save everyone I knew from themselves by getting them to do what I did to get past the gates of Hell. I wanted everyone to feel the peace that I felt. If only they would listen to me!

It didn't take long for me to realize that if someone isn't ready to hear about recovery, and learn about changing and taking risks to improve their life, they aren't going to respond well to my preaching about my own awakening. Just as I had to be desperate enough in my own misery to open my ears to the truth, so do others. When and how they get to that point is not reliant on my telling them.

Today: I will remember that the best way for me to share my message of recovery and peace with others is to live my life in a way that attracts communication and hope.

Grateful To Be Alive

August 4

Many times during my days of active addiction, I thought that killing myself was the answer to all my problems. Today, as I am finding my way through a spiritual journey that has taken my heart to heights of love beyond anything I ever could have imagined, I know that killing myself is the answer to nothing.

I still have bad days, and sometimes horrid days. I still feel sad sometimes and the guilt of past behaviors rumbles to the surface and holds me in chains once again. But even on these not-so-great days, I am still grateful to be alive. And, if I take the time to expand on that gratitude for my life and write down a few other things for which I am grateful, I often forget why I was sad in the first place.

Today: I will remember to focus on gratitude.

Each Moment Is An Opportunity

Anything that happens to me today is an opportunity.

If I am held up in traffic on the way to an important appointment, it is an opportunity for patience.

If I stand behind a complaining customer at the bank, it is an opportunity for tolerance.

If my boss has a different idea about how I should complete a project than I do, it is an opportunity to have an open mind.

If my friend calls and asks me to delay our lunch meeting by an hour, it is an opportunity to be flexible.

If I am told that my cat is in the latter stages of renal failure, it is an opportunity to experience acceptance of my powerlessness.

TODAY: I will remember to focus on the opportunity of the moment, instead of the annoyance of it.

God Loves Me—Yesterday, Today, And Tomorrow

August 6

Every day is a day to become the person God has always wanted me to be. Who I was or what I did yesterday doesn't matter. I can do with today whatever I choose. I can start to become right now, at this very moment.

For a long time, I sat around in self-pity, mulling over the horrors of my past and feeling guilty for the things I had done to cope with it all. I put myself down for being weak and told myself I wasn't worth taking care of.

The constant looking back at yesterday gave me no opening to be hopeful for today. It wasn't until I faced yesterday and recognized it for what it was and who I was while in it, that I was able to move on from it into today. And the me of today is the one God believes in.

Today: I will remember that no matter where I have come from or what I have done, I can be a good person today.

August 7

Weed The Garden And Sleep In Peace

When I am in my mind, turning over resentments, worries, fears, and disappointments, I am tangled in the weeds that hold me back from growth. These weeds that keep me from God, in turn, keep me from myself.

Today I choose to take these weeds, root and all, to a trusted friend—to talk about them and share my feelings about them. I sometimes ask for guidance, and other times just ask to be heard. Either way, I am ridding myself of the toxicity that burns in my soul and will not allow me to rest.

When our talk is finished, I express my gratitude to God for gently pulling these weeds from my grasp by providing me with this understanding friend. I know I will be able to lay my head restfully on my pillow tonight.

Today: I will remember that whatever upset or worried me today that I did not speak of with another, will be the thing that keeps me awake tonight.

Pray And Change

Since the day I was born, God has been by my side, guiding me and offering comfort and love. He has never left me. He has carried me and protected me and accepted every part of me.

I, on the other hand, have turned away from God's guidance. I have slapped away His hugs and wept in my loneliness. I have called out to Him and then questioned the way in which He led me. I have begged Him for mercy and then ignored His forgiveness, thinking I did not deserve it.

When I finally set aside everything I thought I wanted, everything I thought I knew, and truly opened my heart to God in prayer, I stood at the beginning of my transformation. Each day, as I go to Him and ask for my heart to be filled with His will for me, I am growing and changing into a better me. Each day, the change occurs—not because God hears or answers my prayers, but because I pray.

TODAY: I will remember to talk to God—when my eyes first open in the morning, throughout the day, and when I lay my head on my pillow at night. Through these mini conversations with my higher power, I will be opened to experiencing moments of grace.

Recognizing Fear

Because I am human, I cannot deny the fact that I am, at certain times, going to be vulnerable to fear. No matter how much work I do to better myself and no matter how much I pray, fear will always be able to find its way to my heart. Fortunately, because of the strong relationship I have with God today, I can recognize that "flood of fear" when it attempts to consume me. I can lean on the support group of people that I have built up over the years, by talking to them about my fear and asking for help. I can ask for guidance from God and trust that He will not allow the thing I fear to overtake me.

As long as I am alive, fear will exist. I have faith that the strength of my program of recovery and my relationship with God will extinguish fear's spark before it can become a flame.

TODAY: I will remember that when I feel fearful, I am being given an opportunity to have faith. Each time I seize that opportunity, I am closer to God.

Clearing The Hurdles

August 10

I always thought I knew what I wanted. Not only that, but I also thought I knew what was best for the people around me. I did everything I could to make sure I got what I wanted, and others knew exactly what I thought they should be doing. If they didn't give me what I wanted or didn't want to hear my opinions about their life, I simply became manipulative and sneaky in my methods. Needless to say, this formula for living did not make for smooth sailing.

Letting go of everything I thought I knew to open my mind and heart to God's will has given me the freedom to run in life's race without tripping myself or others. I can accept that sometimes I won't come in first place. And I can accept that sometimes other people may just want to sit and watch.

The only thing I can do is make sure I run my leg of the race as best as I can at any given moment. Whether or not a hurdle appears is not up to me. What is up to me is how I approach the hurdle and how I accept my landing after I am past it. Whether I fly effortlessly over it, knock it down on the way over, or land flat on my face because of it, I have faith today that I will be able to continue running the race.

Today: I will remember that when I get out of the way and let God run the show, I find the hurdles in life are much easier to clear.

Living In Reality

When I was trying to figure out what I wanted to be when I grew up, I often thought of becoming an actor.

I think a lot of people who struggle with addiction have this same desire. It seems like a dream job—a job where I get to be someone completely different. I get to pretend I'm someone better, brighter, and more important than I really am—and I get paid for it!

The trouble I see with acting as a profession is that I could probably become addicted to it, just like I am to food and alcohol. The draw to being someone else all the time could feed my need to escape from the real me instead of surrendering to reality and accepting the real me for who I am. For me, it would be one more way to look outside of myself for relief, when I know that looking within has been the only thing to bring me peace.

Today: I will remember that running from myself never brings peace; it only prolongs my discomfort.

A Most Expensive Lie

August 12

How important is it that I am the most successful person I know? How important is it that I have more money than everyone around me? Is being the best, most successful, richest person worth ignoring my own moral code? If I have to lie, cheat, and steal to get to the top of the heap, is it really worth it?

I'm sure there are people in this world who have made it to powerful positions without cheating others. Unfortunately, the ones we often hear about are those who put money and success in front of everything and everyone else in their lives. As much as we're told, through advertising and the like, that having more money will make us happier people, it is all one giant lie.

Money cannot put its arms around me to comfort me when I'm sad. Money cannot sit with me during a crisis and remind me that I'm not alone. Money cannot hold my hand as I walk along the beach and share in my appreciation of God's world. Money cannot turn me into something I am not.

Today: I will remember that I would rather live from paycheck to paycheck than to be known as a "rat"—a person who is more interested in winning than in caring about others.

Worthy Of Risk

It isn't always easy to take a risk. To go out on the first date with someone new, to apply for the job that seems just out of reach, to go to a social event alone—these things, at times, can seem overwhelmingly frightening to me. What if it doesn't work out? What if I am not hired? What if people point at me and laugh because I am alone? The "what ifs" that fill my mind serve only to keep me from stepping out of my comfort zone and taking the risk that might just move me to the next part of my path in life.

But when a relationship doesn't work out, I hate that feeling of loss. When I don't get a job I want, I can't stand feeling rejected. When I'm alone, even in a room full of people, I'm afraid I'll always be alone and never have anyone to love. I sometimes tell myself that those feelings are too much to take. I want to retreat into isolation and protect myself from hurting.

Then I am reminded of the joy my heart feels when I take a risk, and am given back more than I ever could have imagined for myself: the self-respect that comes with knowing I am worthy of that risk, no matter what happens.

TODAY: I will remember that if I avoid relationships, challenges, and love out of the fear of losing, hurting, and grieving, I will be turning my back on life.

Thy Will, Not Mine

As a child, when I didn't get my way, I would cry or stomp away in disgust, showing my disappointment and frustration to anyone nearby. Sadly, as I grew up, I continued to wear my disappointment on my sleeve. I wanted what I wanted and if I didn't get it, you were certainly going to know about it. I may not have thrown a child-like temper tantrum, but I still always insisted on my way. This kind of behavior kept me isolated from others and constantly resentful.

Today, "Thy will, not mine" is one of my favorite prayers. I know that I am not always going to get what I want, and thank God for that! When I look back over my life, I see so many times when I thought I knew what was best for me and for others, and I was so wrong! Had things happened the way I thought I wanted, I may never have found my way to recovery from my addictions—which has been my saving grace.

Today: I will remember that insisting on what I want all the time will separate me from others and from God.

AUGUST 15

Staying Real In Love

Relationships are difficult. Romantic relationships are next to impossible. I can be so confident in many areas of my life, but when it comes to falling in love, I become fragments of myself, littered sparsely throughout my days.

When I think about the really good friends I have in my life today, I remember a very slow getting-to-know-you time after we first met. We didn't spend every waking moment together or talking on the phone; we just got together occasionally and recognized likenesses over time. That's such a rational way to begin a relationship.

Unfortunately, romantic relationships have a much different kind of beginning, and therefore can be more tumultuous at times. Perhaps there is a reason for that, which I do not understand. What I do know is that if I am not my real self—through both smooth and rocky times—I will never be able to truly experience love.

TODAY: I will remember that getting to know someone new can be exhilarating and intoxicating. I can embrace those feelings and enjoy them, but I don't have to let go of who I am in order to do so.

Take A Different Look

August 16

The way I perceive something has a lot to do with how I feel about it. I can look at a blank page of paper and think of how difficult it will be to fill it, or I can see a wonderful opportunity to express my feelings and opinions through writing.

It sounds trite, but it is so true—there is real power in positive thinking. And just as negative thinking breeds more negative thinking, positive thinking breeds more positive thinking. Have you ever tried to sit in self-pity while listening to a motivational speaker? It's just not possible!

Today: I will remember that my perception of things has everything to do with how I feel. If I feel sad, maybe I just need to look at my day in a different way.

AUGUST 17

God's Will Becomes Clear With Action

I can talk a good game. When I was in my late teens, I started talking about the great American novel I was going to write. Through my college years, my twenties, and early thirties, I continued to talk about that novel. I told everyone who would listen that I wanted to be a writer and get paid for it. Occasionally, I would wonder why it wasn't happening for me. I would assume that God just didn't want me to be happy. I never thought it might have something to do with what I was doing—or not doing.

In my late thirties, something inside of me made me sit down to write that novel. Little by little, I put together over twenty chapters. My heart wasn't completely in it—just enough to be able to talk about it with friends and not feel as guilty as when I wasn't writing at all. Along the way, a strange thing happened. I realized through spiritual literature I was reading and studying that I no longer wanted to write that "great American novel." What I wanted was to carry God's message with my writing. I've been doing that ever since.

TODAY: I will remember that I may not be able to see God's will for me if I am not taking action to find my way in the world. What can I do today to take my next step?

Identifying Instead Of Comparing

As soon as I start to think I'm better than someone else, I need to check myself. I need to remember that I may have had more education, or I may have been mentored by the best in the business, but that doesn't make me more important than anyone else. Just because I can answer the most questions during a game of Trivial Pursuit does not give me the right to be condescending to someone who doesn't have a college degree.

Equally, as soon as I start to think that I'm worse than someone else, I need to check myself. I need to remember that my life may have been difficult at times and my family may be extremely dysfunctional, but that doesn't make me more unfortunate than anyone else. Just because my childhood wasn't like that of Beaver Cleaver doesn't give me the right to judge someone else who may be happier than I am.

Today: I will remember that I can't possibly know enough about the life of someone else to place any judgment on them—whether it is better or worse than what I think of myself.

AUGUST 19

Stay Angry, Stay Stuck

Have you ever noticed how exhausting it is to stay angry about something? When I carry anger around all day, nursing it by remembering over and over again whatever caused it, and piling on more resentments as it grows in my heart, I feed the anger and it begins to take over. My mind and body become tired and I begin to feel beat up and self-pitying. I am suspicious of everyone and everything around me. I start using the word "hate" more often when referring to people and things in my life. I lose sight of what is in front of me and become blind to my blessings.

Right now, I feel tired just from writing the previous paragraph. Staying angry about something is not worth it anymore. I can't change what has happened, and I certainly can't change the way people act toward me or react to things I do. All I can do is ask God to guide me in my communication with all people and help me to forgive those who hurt me—knowingly or not.

TODAY: I will remember that feeding my anger only gives it an opportunity to get between me and God. Instead, I will recognize it, talk about it with a friend, and then pray for its release.

Grateful To Be Desperate

August 20

As long as I can remember living, I thought I was weak and pathetic because I couldn't stop myself from overeating. No matter what diet I tried, no matter how much I exercised, no matter how good I felt about myself when I lost weight, I could never keep it off because I always went back to my old overeating behaviors. Sometimes it happened gradually, other times it was immediate—but it always happened.

It wasn't until I was ready to change everything about how I lived in order to feel better that I was able to stop overeating. Even though I had learned everything there was to know about healthy eating, it took feeling absolutely desperate for me to open my mind to the experience of someone else with the same obsession with food who had found a way to stop overeating.

Today: I will remember to be grateful for moments of desperation, for they can bring about marvelous new beginnings if I'm willing to open my heart and soul to a new way of doing something.

August 21

Thank God I Know That I Don't Know

As I look back over times in my life when I was in denial, I am frightened by its power. The first time someone told me they thought I drank too much, I was in high school—maybe fifteen years old. The last time someone told me they thought I drank too much, I was twenty-eight years old. How many times did someone tell me they thought I drank too much between those ages? I can't even count!

While I was drinking during those thirteen years, I lived in denial that I had a problem with alcohol. I lost friends, went home with people I didn't know, drove a car while intoxicated, alienated most of my family, and accrued an enormous amount of debt. None of this seemed like a red flag to me; I was just having fun.

When the veil of denial was finally lifted and I was able to see the wreckage of my life, I was horrified. Slowly, over time, I learned to live a better life, make amends to those I had hurt during my days of drinking, and thank God for keeping me from harm during that time.

Since I stopped drinking, I have also learned that I still don't know a lot about how to live—but at least today I know that I don't know.

Today: I will remember that more will constantly be revealed to me, as long as I stick to clean living.

Willing To Believe

It has been said that the three final consequences of active addiction are jail, institutions, and death. It has also been said that without a relationship with a higher power—of your understanding—you will not be able to recover from addiction.

Rather than risk incarceration, insanity, or death, I'm willing to believe—just for today—that there is a power greater than myself out there in the universe that will save me.

Today: I will remember that since I cannot control the world around me, I may also need a power greater than myself to control the things within me that are hurting me.

AUGUST 23

Don't Fear Responsibility

Being responsible is being true to my word. It is showing up on time, doing things I say I'm going to do, not over-committing myself to a schedule that is impossible to keep, and being honest with myself and those around me about what I need and want.

At times, it can be difficult to voice my honest thoughts about something. When a colleague tells a racist joke in my presence and it offends me, my responsibility is to say something about it. My people-pleasing nature wants me to pretend I thought the joke was funny, or just walk away without saying anything. But my responsibility to myself and to the people around me is to ask that those types of jokes not be told in my presence any more. I may have fear in doing this, but the reward of self-respect that comes from setting responsible boundaries is beyond description.

TODAY: I will remember to set aside fear and move forward with my responsibilities.

It Is All From God

AUGUST 24

My pride often stands as a wall blocking me from the world. When I am walking around, thinking all of my accomplishments are mine and all that I know is because of me, I am treading on very shaky ground. When I "get my fur up" because someone has corrected me or provided a different way of doing something from my own way, I am unrealistically believing that I have all the answers and only my opinions count.

Only God can be credited with what I know or how well I speak in front of any audience. Only God can receive the glory for my recovery from addiction or my ability to forgive. Only God has enough grace to give me when my humanness charges forward with defective characteristics. As soon as I start taking credit for any of it, that's how soon I will lose it all.

TODAY: I will remember that pride is a mask I wear when I serve in order to receive awards and kudos. Grace is God working through me when I serve to live a better life and help another, no matter what the outcome.

AUGUST 25

Listen, Be Open, Learn

"When you think you know everything, it gets in the way of knowing anything."

Rev. Paul E. Clark

How can I hear new ideas when I am always talking? How can I accept a different way of doing something if I think my way is the best way? How can I learn anything when I think I already know everything?

When someone is sharing an opinion with me, instead of thinking of how I will respond when they are finished talking, it is important that I just listen. When someone provides a solution to a problem that is different than my own, it might be a good idea for me to give it a try. And when I am listening to someone who is giving a speech, I must be open to learning something new, no matter how much I think I already know on the topic.

As long as I live, I will never know everything. Today I am open to learning something new or different.

TODAY: I will remember that when I think I have all the answers, that is exactly when I need to stop and ask for help.

I Don't Have All The Answers

August 26

"Plans fail for lack of counsel, but with many advisors they succeed."

Proverbs 15:22, New International Version

I come up with a lot of great ideas when I'm alone in my own mind. I am a master planner, ready to take on the world, to mend all fences, and to alleviate the pain of others.

Most of the time, my motives for these great strategies are good, but there are times when they are grandiose and created to feed my ego. That is why I have no problem calling on my support group of friends to ask for guidance. I simply pick up the phone, ask for an open ear and share my idea. Whether it be to plan a surprise party for my mother's birthday or to go into work and apologize to a co-worker for being snippy at work the previous day, listening to the experience of another just might be helpful to me.

I have learned that it is very often the case that my schemes need to be toned down to adhere to a level of grace that doesn't exist in my own mind. Asking a trusted friend to share their opinion is a good reminder that I don't have all the answers.

Today: I will remember that following through with a plan I have not checked with another may make the need for future amends to arise.

August 27

Talent Needs Risk To Be Recognized

For a long time people told me I was a good writer. Teachers told me I had a talent for putting words together on paper. Friends told me my writing helped them understand certain situations that previously baffled them. It was obvious that I had a talent for forming a message through the keyboard of my computer.

That said, my success with earning a living through writing remained non-existent. Fear of rejection kept me from sending my work to publishers. Fear of the unknown kept me from trying to get a job that would feed my talent.

Fortunately, I realize today that my writing will never be able to help another if I don't risk sharing it—not just with close friends, but with publishers who don't know me and may reject it. I will never be able to find success if I don't try and try and try again to have my talent accepted.

Today: I will remember that I may have been given a talent for writing, but it is helping no one if it is hidden in a notebook on my own bookshelf.

You Can't Think Away The Feelings

I can figure this out. I will find a way to make it work. I know exactly why I do what I do because I've read all about the dysfunctional family unit and the role of each individual family member. I'll come up with a plan to make sure that never happens to me again.

I sure can be a control freak when I start thinking about what's going on around me. I don't ever want to feel sadness or pain, so I get into my mind, climb on the hamster wheel that resides there, and start running. The problem with this method is that I expend an awful lot of energy to get nowhere.

Instead, why don't I just sit still and allow myself to feel whatever it is I'm feeling? Whether it is loneliness or joy, I can accept it and know that I will not feel this feeling forever. Thinking about how to change it will not change it—now or tomorrow. It is only for this moment.

Today: I will remember to ask myself what feeling I'm running from when I catch myself thinking too much about how to change things.

August 29

Easier Isn't Always Better

Did you ever notice how taking care of yourself sometimes means doing things you don't want to do? I can ask why that is, but only God knows the answer. In place of questioning it, I choose to provide myself with examples of times I did something I didn't want to do in order to better myself that ended up giving back to me tenfold:

- Eating a proper diet for the past twelve-plus years has removed high blood pressure and morbid obesity from my medical chart.
- Being responsible at work has provided a consistent and increased paycheck.
- Not using my credit card to buy everything I want has given me a debt-free peace of mind that I never knew was possible.
- Asking for guidance instead of barreling ahead with my anger has saved me from hurting the feelings of a loved one.
- Would it have been easier to eat and buy whatever I wanted, whenever I wanted? Would I be less stressed if I didn't care about work or if I thought only about my own feelings? Maybe. But, for today, I'd rather have peace in my heart than immediate gratification of all my wants.

Today: I will remember that taking care of myself and becoming a better person is not always easy, but it is always worthwhile.

Replace Hate

Hate is such a violent word. It invariably invokes a physical reaction when spoken or thought. It closes doors to potential relationships. It clouds judgment and feeds anger.

Fortunately, hate only has the power to grow in my soul when I feed it. I can look at another and despise them and their behavior, or I can accept that they may be in a painful place on their journey today and are simply acting in the best way that they can at this moment. I can turn away in fear from a person whose beliefs are different than mine, or I can trust that no matter what we all believe, we are all here for a reason, a purpose beyond what I may be able to understand.

Instead of hating, I can accept, trust, and believe that God's world and the people in it are exactly the way they are meant to be.

TODAY: I will remember to pray to God to remove my hatred and replace it with an asset that will enable me to carry His message.

Self-Supporting

Credit cards. Bank loans. Borrowing money from family. Mooching off of friends. Never quite pulling my weight. All this describes how I lived for the first thirty years of my life.

I never felt dignified when I picked up the phone to call my mom and beg for a loan—a "loan" that she and I both knew I would never pay back. I had absolutely no dignity when I was consistently bugging my sister to order take-out and never offered to pay for my share. And I only felt shame while I avoided reaching for the bill when I went out with friends because I knew they would eventually take care of it.

These days, I have a full-time job, checking and savings accounts, and a credit card with a limit that can't be raised. Occasionally I see something I want to buy and I know it's outside my budget for the month. Instead of charging it or using budgeted money for it, I move beyond it and eventually realize that I don't really need it. It's not always easy, but the dignity I feel in being self-supporting feels better than any purchase I could make!

Today: I will remember to ask myself this question the next time I want to buy something: Do I really need it, or do I just want it?

Stop Growing, Start Dying

September 1

My father was a Methodist minister. He was an intelligent man, a wonderful preacher, and had a fantastic sense of humor. He was also afflicted with the disease of alcoholism, which cast a shadow over everything else about him. While he understood and could teach the word of God, his addiction made it impossible for him to live by it.

Today, I remember my father when I conduct myself in a way that is unruly or unfair. I call into mind how it felt to have him pass judgment on me while I watched as he carried God's message through words, but not through his actions. His disease—which I inherited—is a constant reminder that no matter how much I have learned or how much I think I know, my growth depends solely on how I behave on a daily basis.

Today: I will remember that there is no graduation from growing toward God's grace. When I stop growing, I start dying.

SEPTEMBER 2 Relationship With God Equals Happiness

I only recently started to grasp the idea that my happiness lies within me, and not in the actions of those around me. For a long time I thought I'd only be happy if the guy I liked liked me back.

I never listened when teachers told me I had to like myself before anyone else could like me. I thought it was hogwash that anyone who was alone was able to be happy. I thought I had to have the perfect Prince Charming in my life in order to just be okay, let alone happy.

Waiting for someone else to sweep me off my feet was a long and lonely road. It wasn't until I looked within and asked God to show me the way that I was whisked away into a happiness I didn't even know was possible. This state of being relies not on a perfect love from my husband or praise from my boss, but in my relationship with God.

TODAY: I will remember to start the day by talking to God, building upon the relationship with Him that nurtures my happiness.

Have Faith And Move Forward

My world is shattered over and over again, sometimes quietly and sometimes with an enormously loud boom. The shatters happen when something I thought I knew turns out to be false. They happen when a friend cancels a lunch date. They happen when a colleague gets a new job and leaves me behind. They happen when I am betrayed by a loved one. They happen when I stand at the bottom of a dry well with my empty cup and finally recognize that there is not a drop of water in sight.

My faith is what makes my feet move after those shatters—when I accept that I may not have all the answers, when I risk making another lunch date with that friend, when I welcome the new person at work, when I forgive the humans around me, and when I accept the help of the ladder lowered into the well in order to climb out into the light.

My faith is that even though I may not know what will happen next, I will trust it to guide me.

Today: I will remember that relying on my faith is the only way to keep moving forward.

September 4

Stop Pretending

It's risky to be the real me. What if my beliefs don't mesh with someone else's beliefs? What if they don't like me? What if they laugh at me?

No matter where I am, who I am with, or what I am doing, the only way to feel truly at peace is to be myself in any single moment. What I believe, who I love, how I see myself—these things are what I consider my truth. When I am moving in that truth, I am peaceful. When I am holding back because of my fear that tells me I'm not good enough, pretty enough, smart enough, etc., I am uncomfortable, disjointed, and anxious. How I walk through each day is up to me.

Today: I will remember that trying to get other people to like me by being someone I'm not or saying something I don't believe is not a risk I am willing to take.

Listen And Trust God

My best friends are wonderful listeners. They look at me when I'm talking to them. They don't interrupt me by answering their cell phones or shushing me when something good comes on television. I can tell that they care about what I'm saying by how still they are while I'm talking.

I find this characteristic very attractive. I want to be a good listener. I want to be a good friend. I want to be helpful and calm for others. Unfortunately one of my greatest character limitations is when someone else is talking to me and I am missing most of what they are saying because I'm thinking about how I'm going to respond. Even merely thinking while another is talking is focusing on something other than that person's sharing.

There is only one way for me to overcome this limitation. I need to ask God to take it from me. I need to trust that He will give me whatever words I may need when another is finished talking to respond with grace and respect.

TODAY: I will remember that I help others only when I open my heart and soul to God's grace. As soon as I start thinking about the best response, that is how soon I have cut myself off from His guidance.

Try And Try Again

For today, I will get out of bed, say my prayers, kiss my spouse good-bye, and be on my way. I will accept everything as it comes and keep from judging others. I will face fear when it comes and keep my head up when I feel discouraged. I will give what I can and provide comfort to others when it is needed. I will speak kindly to the check-out girl and let someone go in front of me in traffic. I will be grateful for all of the blessings in my life and not want for anything outside my means. I can do this.

This is a great objective and one that I strive for on a daily basis. But in spite of this, I am human and therefore imperfect. On any given day, the best I can be may not have anything to do with the ideas mentioned in the paragraph above. My best might be to retreat to the bathroom at work when I'd rather ream out a colleague for making their lack of planning my emergency. Or it might be to clench my teeth shut and say nothing instead of being rude to someone who cuts in front of me in line at the post office. And, it may be crying on the phone to a friend because I'm afraid of losing my job or failing a class.

No matter what my best is today, as long as I'm trying I can rest my head on the pillow tonight in peace, knowing that tomorrow will give me another try.

TODAY: I will remember that on some days my best is better than on others. The good news is that as long as I'm trying to be my best, it has to be better than my worst.

In The Curve

September 7

Sometimes I can't see past my own reach. Not just physically, but emotionally and spiritually as well. It might be because I'm hurting from a lost love or angry about the unnecessary suffering in the world. Or it might be because I'm afraid to trust that God has my best interests in mind as He is carrying out His plan.

Whatever the reason, there are times when I find myself at a place I refer to as "in the curve." Just like when I'm driving and I enter a sharp curve, I can't see anything other than the road immediately in front of me. I have to have faith that as I continue through the turn, there will be a road in front of me. I have to slow down in order to avoid crashing into obstacles I cannot yet see. And I have to believe that wherever I am when the road has finished bending will be exactly where I'm supposed to be.

Today: I will remember that when I'm "in the curve" I need to pay attention to the signs around me, relax my grip on the wheel, and allow myself to be guided by the path ahead.

Living The Life I Choose

I once heard someone say, "You're a victim until you're eighteen; after that you're a volunteer." At the time, this statement really offended me—probably because I spent the majority of my young adult life blaming everyone around me for how bad I felt about myself.

What I take from that person's words is the idea that whatever I am doing today as a grown woman, I am choosing to do it. Whether I like my job or not, I am choosing to get out of bed and show up at work. If I am lonely and feel isolated from the world, it is because of choices I have made that have cut me off from friends and family.

It isn't always easy to break away from feeling victimized. In fact, after spending an entire childhood growing up in a dysfunctional family, it can feel impossible. But it's not. All I have to do is make one choice today that allows me to be responsible for myself and my feelings. It might be as simple as choosing to find gratitude in my work instead of complaining about it. Or it might mean updating my resume to apply for the job I really want. Either way, it's my choice.

Today: I will remember that my choices have gotten me where I am today. If I don't like where I am, I can choose to change it—one step at a time.

Recognizing Good In Others

I have never wanted to excel in my job when I worked for people who didn't appreciate my skills and commitment. I was unable to develop my talents growing up in a home filled with abuse and dysfunction.

However, when I find myself surrounded by people who understand and accept me, and love and appreciate me anyway, I feel a strong desire to become the best person I can possibly be.

I must remember when I am working with others—whether it be on a volunteer committee, at work, or in my daily personal encounters—that my relationships and successes will best be served as I express gratitude and applaud the accomplishments of those around me.

Today: I will remember to openly recognize the good in others.

September 10

Ignorant And Proud Of It

For a long time I thought I had to know everything—my future, the world, how the people around me should act. Little hamsters ran on their wheels inside my mind at a rapid pace, trying to figure it all out. I pretended I knew what you were talking about when I really had no idea. I acted like I understood more than the people around me so they would be impressed by me. It was exhausting.

I can't say exactly when it happened or how, but there is one thing I know for certain today: I don't have all the answers. Thank God! What a relief it is to say, "I don't know." How free it feels to ask for help when I'm confused or have lost my way. What a blessing to rely on the experiences of those who have gone before me to guide me in my next steps. How grateful I am each time I refrain from pretending and show you the real me—ignorance and all.

Today: I will remember that knowing that I don't know makes me a whole lot smarter than pretending I do.

Just Do One Thing Today

Procrastination was once a huge character defect that held me back from living my life. Whether faced with a problem or potential success, I procrastinated. I was afraid that I wouldn't be able to handle whatever came next, be it failure, pain, or achievement.

During the past few years, I have learned that once I acknowledge my own procrastination, all I need to do is take one tiny step each day to overcome it. For example, if I have been procrastinating making amends to an old college friend, I can take just one step toward doing so today by writing down what I might say or do to make those amends. I don't have to pick up the phone, see that person, or make the actual amends today. All I need to do is put a pen to paper and straighten out my own thoughts regarding the issue.

So often I don't confront problems or tasks because I am looking at the big picture, everything I will have to do to get to the other side of it. But when I stay in the moment and recognize the simplicity of one simple step toward solving or completing it, I am empowered.

TODAY: I will remember to think only of the next step I need to take, instead of the marathon that may be in front of me.

How To Use A Bad Mood

Since I've been working toward becoming a better person on a daily basis, peace and serenity have made their way into my heart, and therefore into many moments of my days. It has felt wonderful to be respectful of others while also respecting my own wants and needs. I have found relief in following the path God has set before me, and joy in the rewards of open and honest communication with the people in my life.

However, sometimes—due to no particular thing, person, or event—I wake up in the morning with a sour attitude, which tries to creep into every moment of my day. What I do with this sour attitude, when I feel like doing nothing with it but feeding it, is what most defines my character. Do I act out on my crankiness or do I pause and ask God to relieve me of my worst and replace it with His best? The answer is simple if I'm willing to humbly embrace my humanness.

TODAY: I will remember that a bad mood doesn't need to ruin my day. In fact, if I treat it properly, it will serve to bring me closer to God and becoming the person I was meant to be.

Refrain From Attacking With Honesty

September 13

I've heard it said by many that to be honest with each other is what aids most in building strong relationships. For when we are honest, there are no secrets, no miscommunications, no spaces of the unknown that lie between us and build walls of fear and uncertainty.

While I believe honest and open communication is important, I also know that when I become ready to "attack" with truth, I need to check myself and my motives. Am I being honest because I want to improve my relationship with someone, or because I am feeling resentful and ignored and subconsciously want to hurt that person? Am I exposing a truth because it will help strengthen my relationship with someone, or because it will ease my own guilt and shame about a past infraction?

There are many good reasons to be honest. There are also many good reasons to ask myself how it may feel to hear the honesty I have to present.

Today: I will remember that sharing honestly should be graceful, not hurtful.

September 14

Stop Thinking, Start Acting

There are times when I can work myself up into a frenzy of dread and doubt before I'm even close to a certain obligation or event. I think of all the things that could go wrong and all the stupid comments I might make. I remember all the times I have embarrassed myself in the past and I'm certain I will do the same this time around. I worry about how other people will perceive me and if they will like me or not. I think, I remember, and I worry.

Paralyzed by fear is no way to go through life. It's time for me to stop thinking so much and start acting on faith. Only in trusting the path before me will I ever be able to enjoy life, revel in the joys of the moment, and act with confidence.

Today: I will remember to stop thinking so much and start acting as if I believe it will all turn out for the best.

Leaving The Comfort Zone

September 15

For a very long time, I had a hard time stepping outside of my comfort zone. When I have been called on to learn something new or look deep within to find the parts of me that needed to be changed, I recoiled as if from a hot flame. I felt scared that I wouldn't be smart enough or strong enough and would end up looking silly or falling flat on my face.

After working through this discomfort many times over in order to remain recovered from my addictive behaviors, I have recognized the importance of leaving my comfort zone. Now when I feel uncomfortable, it is usually because I am carrying out a healthy action that I never would have been able to carry out when I was in my active addictions. Because it is new for me to be healthy, it feels uncomfortable. This now serves as a good sign for me. I can embrace it and be present in the discomfort, knowing that I am learning, growing, and changing into the person I was always meant to be.

Today: I will remember to accept my discomfort and be grateful that I am sane enough and clear enough to learn and grow in spite of it.

Today's Purpose

I have spent a lot of time waiting to be happy. Mainly because I thought I couldn't be happy unless I was doing exactly what I wanted to do. Part of the problem was that for most of my life, I really didn't know what it was that I wanted to do. Then, when I realized I needed to face my addictions and all the troubles they had caused in my life, I could see no way to find the time to do what I wanted to do while also focusing on my recovery program full-time—as well as working forty hours per week.

Today I have a good idea of what I would like to be doing to earn a living, and I've made a commitment to work toward that one day at a time. It will take time to get there, but as long as I stay loyal to my dream, I can be at peace with however it turns out. In the meantime, I have discovered something that has lifted the cloud of not getting what I want. I have discovered that what I want to do is to carry out God's will for me. So every day that I am asking Him to guide me and paying attention to whatever is right in front of me, I am doing exactly what I want!

TODAY: I will remember that there is a purpose in focusing on whatever is right in front of me.

Focusing On Changing The World Is Exhausting

It can be utterly exhausting to hold onto a resentment I have toward someone. I feel drained when I allow myself to become exasperated over someone else's behavior. I grow weary and depressed when I spend my days and nights thinking about all the things that could possibly go wrong in the world around me.

All of these things share a common thread: They are outside influences that I take in and allow to control my reactions and emotions. There is nothing I can do about the behaviors of the people around me or whether or not the earth will continue to rotate. The only thing I can do anything about is how I behave and how I react to the world around me. Thinking otherwise will serve only to make me tired.

TODAY: I will remember that when I start worrying about something, or judging the behaviors of others, I am setting myself up for fatigue and doubt.

September 18

Perception Is Nine-Tenths Of Peace

I have heard many women complain about being taken for granted by their husbands and children. From time to time, I have been irritated by my husband's seemingly self-centered behavior in our marriage. I ask him what he wants for dinner and he aloofly says, "Whatever." When I see his dirty clothes on the floor by the door of our bedroom, reminding me to take them to the dry-cleaner, I feel frustrated and offended. When I'm the only one focused on recognizing birthdays, anniversaries, and other special occasions of our family and friends, I feel lonely.

But what if I look at my husband's behavior in a different way? Perhaps he doesn't tell me what he wants for dinner because he trusts that whatever I choose to make for him will satisfy his hunger and tastes. Maybe he leaves the dry-cleaning on the floor because he considers me reliable and efficient. He could be letting me take care of buying gifts and making arrangements to get together with friends and family because he knows that I coordinate our schedules better than he does.

Once again, I am reminded that how I look at something makes a huge difference in how I feel about it.

Today: I will remember to take the time to think about the good in how someone treats me.

Soar, Don't Wallow

September 19

Most people want to be the best they can be. We all strive for success each day of our lives. I long to find contentment and happiness as I travel through life. Approval and acceptance from society add feathers to my wings and give me the courage to take flight. I want to achieve something and thrive among friends.

And yet, there is something inside me that pulls me toward wallowing in the muck of life. The discouraging remarks from others about my dreams, the heartache over lost relationships, the lousy weather on days when I planned to be outside, the dysfunction of my family of origin, the lack of trust in God's plan for me—these are the muddy things of my days that I have used to stay stuck in the muck of disappointment. Regrettably, if I stay there long enough I begin to enjoy it; in fact, I wallow in it. This is a dangerous place for me to stay, and a signal that I need to ask for help in stepping out of the muck that will eventually turn to quicksand.

Today: I will remember that on days when I feel less like soaring through the air and more like wallowing in the mud, I need to call a trusted friend and ask for help.

September 20

Don't Miss Out On Pretty For Busy

Recently, I arrived home from work feeling overwhelmed with job and family responsibilities. After retrieving the mail from the mailbox, I rushed up my driveway, sorting through letters, catalogs, and bills. Out of the corner of my eye, I caught sight of the color yellow. I stopped and turned my attention away from the mail and toward the yellow. There stood a vibrant new daffodil popping out from its roots. The daffodil seemed to smile at me—no worries attached to it, no responsibilities to tend to. In fact, it didn't even show a trace of self-consciousness for springing up at the beginning of autumn when it wasn't even supposed to be there. It was just there being bright and pretty. Perhaps I was meant to see the daffodil and learn from it.

Today: I will remember that when I am caught up in my busyness, I am missing the bright and pretty parts of life.

I Just Am

September 21

When I was a little kid, people were always asking me what I wanted to be when I grew up. I would say, "a teacher" or "a nurse" because that's what I thought little girls were supposed to want to be when they were grown-up mommies. I didn't really want to be a teacher or a nurse—or even a mommy—but I did want to give the answer I thought people wanted to hear.

There is a beautiful freedom in not knowing where my path is taking me today. I just wake up in the morning and step out with faith that I'll be led in the direction that best fits with my talents, desires, needs, and enthusiasm. I don't pretend that I want to be anything I don't want to be. I don't act as if I know things that I don't know. And I don't hide who I really am to make other people happy. I just am.

Today: I will remember that just because I don't know where I'm headed with my life doesn't mean I don't know who I am.

SEPTEMBER 22

No Need To Explain

No explanation is necessary. A person who doesn't need to convince others that what he is doing is acceptable by explaining all the reasoning behind it is a person who is truly at peace. He simply goes about his business, allowing his actions to attract and entice others. He doesn't need approval or permission; he walks along trusting what he has learned to carry him through each moment, each day. Therein lies the beauty of a person who lives harmoniously with the world around him.

TODAY: I will remember that as long as I am acting with dignity and grace, and showing respect for myself and others, there is no need to explain anything I do today.

Comfortable With Me

September 23

For a long time I thought I could only be beautiful if I had the prettiest hair or the perfect face. What I have realized over time is that I could have the most stunning physical features and still not be beautiful. What I feel about myself is what makes me beautiful. Through a daily commitment to check my behaviors, atone for my mistakes, and make living amends through honest and clean living, I leave behind the guilt and shame I carried about myself in the past.

Today the person I see when I look in the mirror is what makes me beautiful. The fact that I can even look at myself in the mirror is a true testament to the power of truly searching and trying to do God's will by staying clean and sober.

Today: I will remember that what other people think of me doesn't matter nearly as much as what I think of myself.

September 24

Replace Complaints With Prayer

If it's going to rain, it's going to rain—there's nothing I can do about it. It's that simple. And just as sitting around whining about a rainy day isn't going to change the weather, when I sit around and whine about something going on in my life, I don't change my circumstances. Until I get up and take action, my whining serves only as an annoyance to the people within earshot.

Complaining is worrying out loud. Worrying is, as we all know, as useless as an electric stove when the power is out. Since I have found serenity in replacing my worries with faith, why not replace my complaints with prayer?

Today: I will remember to pause and pray before I voice a complaint.

Letting Go Of My Plans And Accepting God's Will

Marry Prince Charming and live in a castle built out of chocolate—this was once my plan. It would have been silly for me to grow into a mature adult and hold on to that plan at the same time. It was necessary for me to accept the reality of life—that there is no such thing as Prince Charming and a house made out of chocolate is not practical.

So why is it so difficult for me to let go of the rest of my plans and accept God's design for my life? Why don't I trust that He will show me how and when to act, where and when to walk, and what to say when I get where I'm going? My free will wants to stick out its chest with false pride and interrupt God's progress in my life—that's why. It is only when I recognize this impediment and discard it that I am able to step out onto the path that has always been paved for me.

TODAY: I will remember that my plans are limited by my human understanding. Only God knows what is best for me as I travel through life. Today, I will trust His grace to lead me to my destiny.

September 26

Marriage Is A Journey, Not A Fairytale

Like the journey of life, the journey of a marriage has many twists and turns, ups and downs, and bumps in the road. In order to remain together in the same vehicle, a couple must practice patience, understanding, acceptance, and unconditional love. This is a tall order, and not something I thought about when I was experiencing the bliss of falling in love with my husband. I imagined all the days of my future would be filled with flowers and sunshine—no gray days and certainly never any rain.

Unfortunately, when two human beings share their lives, they are bound to encounter some rough moments. There are times when I experience a spiritual growth spurt, but my husband is stuck in the mud of a resentment he can't shake. And there are days when he is content and serene and I am as moody as ever! These are times when we need to accept each other exactly where we each are on the journey. For it is after the storm that the sun shines the brightest.

Today: I will remember to accept and love my husband for the man he is at this moment.

Praying For Others Changes Me

September 27

It has been suggested to me that when I am angry with someone, I pray for that person for two weeks straight. I pray for them all the blessings I desire for myself. I pray for them even if I don't mean it. I say the words and trust that God will understand my contradictory feelings. At the end of those two weeks, my anger will be gone.

The first time this method was suggested to me, I just about laughed out loud. I couldn't even imagine praying for the person I was angry with at the time. But out of respect for the person making the suggestion, I kept my doubt to myself and followed her direction. Amazingly enough, before the two weeks were past, my anger had dissolved into a murky memory.

To this day, whenever I begin to pray for someone with whom I am angry, I can't believe that it will help. Yet it never fails that through these prayers, God lifts the anger from me. How He does it, I don't know—and I don't need to know. I'm just grateful He does.

Today: I will remember to pray for those who anger me.

SEPTEMBER 28 Love, No Matter What

It can be so difficult to love someone who isn't acting in the manner I think is best for them. While I want to be accepting and forgiving, it hurts me deeply to see someone I love in pain due to their own actions. I want to step in and fix things for them. I want to make it better, show them the way, and tell them what to do in order to feel better. The reality is that what I want is to control them, not love them.

When I feel this way, it is important to remember that the person I love has a higher power, and it is not me. I have no control over how someone acts, or how someone cares—or doesn't care—for themselves. All I can do is ask their higher power to guide them toward the light and grant me the ability and willingness to love them unconditionally. That is the only way I can truly accept and embrace my loved ones.

TODAY: I will remember to express love even to those who behave in ways that make loving difficult, for that is when they are most in need of it.

Human Beings Feel Sad Sometimes

September 29

Some days are blue days. Maybe because it's raining or maybe because the job I hoped would work out, didn't. It doesn't really matter why; some days are just blue, and that's okay.

I always thought I had to numb myself on those blue days. I couldn't stand feeling sad or uncomfortable. I tried to medicate with food, alcohol, drugs, men, shopping—whatever I could get my hands on to make the feeling go away. What inevitably happened was that I ended up feeling worse than just blue. I ended up feeling guilty or ashamed by my behavior and the original blue-ness that I felt became a deep and dark depression.

It is only through truly feeling a feeling that I can gain from it. Whether it be blue-ness or joy, I must allow myself to experience it in order to learn from it.

Today: I will remember that I am blessed with a plethora of feelings; to ignore any of them or try to wash them away would be to turn my back on living.

September 30

Connecting To God Is A Daily Need

On many days, the world can be as tough as a boxing match. How I prepare myself to step into the ring each day is what gives me the courage to face whatever may be thrown my way.

When I pray for guidance in the morning and open my heart willingly to God's path, my steps in the ring of life are usually smooth and swift. But when I forget to pray before I leave the house for the day, I will most likely be tripping over one or more of my character defects before it is even lunchtime.

I experience an indescribable peace when my communication with God is consistently honest and honestly consistent.

Today: I will remember that in order to dance under the lights of life, I need to consistently connect with God.

Act As If...

"Act as if." This is a phrase I often hear in reference to taking action to make a change, even when I don't believe in the change or the action. It tells me that if I "pretend" to believe in what I'm doing, I eventually will believe.

At times I have a difficult time embracing this concept. I want concrete answers in front of me that I can trust. I want to be able to know that something is going to help me before I spend any time doing it. What I have come to realize is that life doesn't work that way.

Sometimes I just have to act on faith. Sometimes I need to trust the people around me and follow their suggestions, even if I don't believe in them. In doing this, it has been proven to me time and time again that just following through with the action—whether I believe in it or not—will change how I feel. That change in feeling then guides me to release from fear, desperation, depression, sadness, hopelessness—whatever I am feeling that drove me to act. And that release is the best concrete evidence I could ever have.

Today: I will remember that taking action to change will serve abundantly to remove the dark clouds of despair that follow me.

October 2

Smile When You Need It

I love surprise smiles. When a smile sneaks up on me, I feel my entire soul awaken. This isn't how I feel when someone is pointing a camera at me and telling me to smile. It isn't how I feel when I'm in a bad mood and someone tells me to smile because it increases my face value. It happens only when my true self finds pleasure in something or someone. It is a gift that comes when I allow myself to express joy and wonder. And that gift is only presented to me when I am at peace with who I am.

Today: I will remember that a true smile is one that needs no audience.

I Show Others How To Treat Me By How I Treat Myself

I once heard someone say, "No one can use you as a doormat unless you are already lying on the floor." That image pounded home to me the fact that we show others how we are willing to be treated by how we respect ourselves and our own needs.

If I never stand up for myself, why would anyone expect me to say no when they want me to say yes? If I don't value my own opinions, why would anyone else give thought to what I have to say? If I don't take care of my own needs, why would others care if I am fulfilled or not?

It is in my own best interest to find the self-respect I need to carry myself through each day with dignity and grace. It isn't always an easy thing to do, because when I am taking care of myself I can't always please everyone. But, it is a guarantee that all my relationships will be improved when I am able to be honest about my needs.

Today: I will remember that when I allow others to use me by not sharing my true feelings, I have no one to blame but myself.

Blah, Blah, Blah

Every now and then my whining and complaining gets on my own nerves, my soapbox lectures make me want to crawl out of my own skin, and I bore the crap out of myself with too much advice, too much opinionated garble, and too much yapping!

These are times when I need to stop talking, explaining, and expressing myself and just listen. It doesn't even matter if no one else is talking. At these times I need to be quiet. I need to rest within myself and allow the world to speak to me. I need to absorb the messages that flow through the day before I can carry them in my heart to others.

TODAY: I will remember that listening is a beautiful skill. Truly hearing what the world has to say is a gift I can only give when I'm not concerned with myself.

Strength In Unity

October 5

Try to break a stick in half. Then put that stick together with another and try to break the pair of them in half. You will notice that if you continue to add sticks, one at a time, to the group, the bundle becomes more and more difficult to break apart. At some point, your collection of sticks will not even bend. Their strength lies in their unity.

It is also so with the people in my life. Whether I am trying to recover from an addiction or plan a big project at work, I have more strength in the unity I find with the people around me. Those other addicts who are trying to recover give me guidance and strength that I could never find from walking the path on my own. My co-workers share ideas and help carry the details of a project, leaving me to concentrate on what's in front of me instead of trying to do everything and becoming stressed and over-worked.

In trusting the experience of others and sharing responsibilities, I am unified, and therefore strengthened.

Today: I will remember to look for things I have in common with others, rather than separating myself from them through our differences.

October 6 The Next Right Thing

I never had any self-esteem when I was running around caring only about myself and acting like an immature brat. I was extremely low on pride when I didn't show up on time for work or give my best each day at the office. And I certainly couldn't find any personal satisfaction in not following through with commitments I had made to myself and others.

Doing the next right thing may sometimes involve the risk of having others dislike me. Other times it may mean that I have to hold to a boundary that someone else just doesn't understand. Most times, it means taking steps that are uncomfortable because I'm responding or acting in a healthy way instead of my old, dysfunctional ways. Whatever the case, the "next right thing" always has a payoff that is beyond anything I could imagine.

Today: I will remember that while my newer, healthier behaviors may sometimes be difficult to carry out or unpopular with the people around me, they are always worth my efforts and energy in the long run.

Wanting Opens The Door To Willingness

October 7

I have needed to recover from my food addiction from the time I was in my early teens—and maybe even before that! But, it wasn't until I was desperate enough to set aside everything I thought I knew about calories, exercising, healthy eating, fat grams, and weight management that I began to want to learn more about recovery from food addiction. And once I started to want to learn, I became more teachable. In other words, my mind opened to new ideas and potential future paths that once were out of the question in my mind.

Similarly, I cannot make someone want to do something. It isn't until a person comes to desire something themselves that they become willing to do whatever it takes to reach that something. Many people need recovery from one thing or another, but it only takes hold when they want it.

Today: I will remember that I can't want something enough for someone else to achieve it. Their own want is what will carry them to it.

OCTOBER 8

Just Go For It

I'm tired of allowing my fear to stop me from following my dreams. I'm tired of worrying that I'm not good enough. I'm tired of listening to the message that tells me I have to be perfect in order to succeed. I'm tired of being concerned about what other people will think of me if I fail. I'm tired of being afraid to fail.

How important is the outcome when I can never even get to it because of my fears? It means nothing if I don't even allow myself to try. How long do I have to sit idly by and watch my life pass over me before I jump onto the journey and take the risk—whatever it is at the moment? How tired of missing out on opportunities do I have to become before I wrap my hands around the next one and let it take me where I'm supposed to go?

Is today the day where going for it has become more important than the outcome?

TODAY: I will remember that not taking a risk may be just as risky to the possible outcome of my life as taking it may be.

Insignificant To One May Mean The World To Another

October 9

Many times when I sit down and write out a gratitude list at the end of my day, things like this show up:

- The pink flowers along the highway that brightened my mood on the way to work…
- The purr of my cat as she sat beside me during my morning meditations…
- The woman who chased me out of the supermarket with an item that had fallen from my cart…

These things may not be influencing the tides, but they are important to me. They brought me comfort, peace, or love at some point during my day, and that alone changes my world.

Today: I will remember to notice the importance of the things and people who cross my path throughout the day.

Being Present

When I am growing in a relationship with someone—whether it be my spouse, a friend, a family member, or fellow employee—I need to be present. This doesn't just mean that I need to show up physically. Yes, I need to spend time with them, attend events that are important to them, and make sure I am available to support them in times of trouble.

But this also means that I need to listen when the other person speaks. I need to recognize the feelings of that person and value their opinions. I need to share my experiences, hopes, dreams, and ideas with them with a genuinely honest and open spirit.

In the physical presence, the emotional availability, and the spiritual connection, I strengthen my bond with another. That bond will not hold if any one of those three is absent.

Today: I will remember to be present for others today—physically, emotionally, and spiritually.

Graceful Persistence

October 11

When I am consistently asked to edit a project at work, or when I feel like I never say anything intelligent, I often feel like throwing up my hands and walking away from it all. It's too hard. I don't have the energy to keep trying to get it right. But something else subsequently speaks to me and tells me to try again.

So I redo the project and I continue to contribute to conversations at work, with friends, and with my family. I trust that I will learn from this process and eventually be led to produce my best work and share the ideas that others need to hear.

Graceful persistence is a fantastic attribute. To keep on keeping on when it seems like nothing is going right for me is something I have only been able to do since living my life free of my addictions. It is one of the greatest gifts that has been granted to me through living cleanly and working toward bettering myself.

Today: I will remember to try again, even when I don't want to. The next thing I do or say may just be exactly what God has planned.

October 12

Listen To The Inner Voice

With his angelic voice and unmatched abilities to entertain a crowd of people, singer Johnny Mathis has been given the gift of doing what he loves most and getting paid for it. Today one might look at his life and think it unfair that he has so much wealth and admiration. Then it needs to be asked: How did he get where he is today?

How could a person who had originally planned to be a physical education teacher find his way away from a try-out for the Melbourne Olympics and to the stage where he would thrill audiences with his voice for the next fifty-plus years? He simply followed the inner instinct that told him to take a chance with his singing.

What if he had doubted that inner voice or his talent? What if he had turned his back on what he loved to do for something that society deemed more appropriate for him? The world would have been robbed of the gifts God intended he share.

Today: I will remember to listen to the inner voice that tells me to follow my dreams and take risks. "Chances Are" the risk will lead me to being blessed with doing what I love every day of my life.

A Lashing Of The Tongue Often Leaves Deeper Scars Than A Lashing With A Belt

I once heard that the Greek root of the word "sarcasm" actually means, "to tear the flesh." This violent image might just be what I need to remember the next time I think it's funny to point out a defect or imperfection in someone else by being sarcastic.

I don't like how I feel when someone else makes fun of me or jokes about something that I am trying to better about myself. I can feel my self-esteem dwindle when I am teased or mocked, even if it is "in jest."

So why would I communicate with anyone else in this way? Perhaps because it seems easier to joke about something that I don't want to be honest about. Sometimes the honesty I need to share with someone feels too difficult to be serious about. Even so, does that justify hurting someone else's feelings through caustic and stinging observations?

TODAY: I will remember that my words have the ability to "tear the flesh" of another. Maybe it would be better to say nothing than to utter a biting remark.

October 14

Compromise Breeds Strength

Even though I was raised by parents who fought with each other consistently, I still thought that when I grew up and found my husband, we would live "happily ever after" just because we were in love.

Love is a powerful thing, but it does not shield me from disappointment, hurt feelings, and the most popular relationship deterrent, self-centeredness. Too often my feelings are hurt or I become disappointed because I don't get my way. Many times I find myself angry and frustrated because my self-centeredness blinds me from the bigger picture that reaches beyond my own selfish desires.

While it is necessary to be true to myself and my individual needs, it is important for me to remember that in any marriage, unity is strength. Only through the willingness to compromise will any union ever succeed.

Today: I will remember that compromising is not "giving in" or "being a doormat." A true compromise gives union and strength to both parties in any relationship.

Pull The Weeds And Plant Flowers

For so long, I walked around believing the messages of my childhood: "I'm not good enough or pretty enough." "I'm not smart enough to be successful." "Men only want women for sex and can't be trusted." "I'm not worthy of God's love." It was exhausting to live in fear of my past.

It wasn't until I reached down into the muck of my past, pulled up the roots of those messages, and called them out for what they were that I was able to move beyond them to messages of inner peace and self-acceptance. It was hard work to call those weeds by name. It changed the way I looked at my childhood and my family of origin. It made the physical, sexual, and emotional abuse, the verbal slayings of an active alcoholic, and the abandonment of all values and moral attitudes real. There was no more room for denial.

Because my trusted friends taught me how to fill those empty spaces of dirt with fertilizers of love, hope, and faith, there was also no more room for weeds to grow. Now those fertilizers feed the beauty of new, healthy plants and flowers that fill my heart today.

Today: I will remember that being honest about past messages and the fears that once ruled my behaviors is the best way to move beyond them.

OCTOBER 16

Nature Brings Comfort

As a child I sat under the honeysuckle bush by the side of our house. In my teen years I joined sports teams that played outdoors. In college I walked to the lake on campus and watched the ducks, geese, and swans glide smoothly over the surface of the water. And in my twenties, as I struggled through the most gripping years of my active addictions, I wrote poetry about the softness of autumn leaves and the peace found only in the center of a daisy.

Nature has always made me feel connected somehow. For a while I tried to analyze it, but now I don't care why or how or when it became a comfort for me. Now when I'm struggling with some part of my life, I just accept that I will feel better, lighter, or more peaceful if I go for a walk outside, sit in the sun, or watch squirrels chase each other through the trees.

TODAY: I will remember to say "hi" to the daffodils before rushing about with my daily tasks.

God Is My Witness

October 17

What if I approached everything in my life as something I am doing for God? Would I still engage in gossip with my friends? Would I insist on arguing with my husband, trying to convince him that I am right and he is wrong? Would I walk past the homeless man on the street, pretending I don't see him?

If I am truly and honestly seeking to do all for God, knowing He would be reviewing my work at the end of each day, I am pretty sure I would go about completing tasks and engaging in relationships much differently than I do on a regular basis.

Today: I will remember to ask myself in all areas of my life, "How would I behave, react, act, and speak if God were standing right beside me?"

October 18

Protecting Myself

"But now I am writing you that you must not associate with anyone who calls himself a brother but is sexually immoral or greedy, an idolater or a slanderer, a drunkard or a swindler. With such a man do not even eat."

1 Corinthians 5:11, New International Version

When I first laid down my addictions, I often heard from others who were recovering that I should "hang with the winners." I also heard that, in order to stay free of my addictions, I may need to change a lot of the "people, places, and things" in my life.

This was difficult stuff to absorb. I thought I could be friends with anyone and still remain clean, as long as I didn't pick up my addictive substances, one day at a time. But what I recognized was that behaviors that were no longer acceptable for me to adopt were also unacceptable to me when they were carried out by others. And when I allow myself to remain in the presence of unacceptable behavior, I find myself quickly beginning to rationalize how that behavior isn't so bad. Therein lies the danger of associating with people who are behaving in ways that have only ever led me to picking up my addictive substances in order to black out the guilt and shame they bring.

Today: I will remember that because I am human, I am vulnerable to the behaviors and attitudes of those around me. The longer I allow myself to be in the presence of unacceptable behaviors, the more likely I will be to accept those behaviors.

Truly Grateful For Honest Criticism

October 19

No one likes to be corrected. No one likes to be told that the way they are doing something may not be the best way to go about doing it. Our egos bruise so easily when a personal fault or defect is recognized.

While I am among those who agree with the above statements, I also know that without honest criticism from those who love and respect me, I would never be able to grow and change into a better person.

It wasn't until my older sister came to me and told me she thought I was an alcoholic that the walls of my denial began to break. I wasn't thrilled with what she said and was pretty angry with her. But when I look back on that moment, sitting in my living room, listening to the words she uttered that I thought were so hurtful, I realize that I had never been loved more honestly by anyone in my life.

Today: I will remember that opening my soul to honest criticism from those who care about me may be the greatest gift I can give myself today.

October 20

Everyone Has Been Hurt

I need to remember that everyone I come across today has a backstory. And as we all sadly know, most backstories involve some amount of pain. Whether the pain others carry is from recent events in their lives or embedded deep in past experiences, it may be a heavy load. Their attitudes toward life and their attitudes toward the peace and love that I feel in my heart may not be warm or engaging. I must not take that personally.

Everyone has experienced rough roads in life. Everyone has had his or her heart broken, or his or her dreams stomped at one time or another. Some people move beyond the hurt better than others. Who am I to judge anyone else's process?

Whether they behave in a way that deserves respect or not, the best I can do today for anyone I encounter is to treat them respectfully.

Today: I will remember to accept others exactly where they are. Expecting anyone to be beyond their own process is setting them up to disappoint me.

No Regrets, Only Gifts

October 21

Information gathered from my past has helped build me into the person I am today. No matter what has happened to me, no matter what I have done without thinking of the consequences, no matter how stupid or intelligent or insane or rational I have been, it has all taught me something I have needed to learn.

At a point in my life when I was having a difficult time making a decision, a good friend told me that if I pray about it and ask God to show me the way—and then listen to His answer as best as I am able, and move forward, continuing to request His guidance along the way—then there will be no right or wrong about my decision. In His grace, I will learn from it, whether it is an easy or difficult lesson doesn't matter.

Today: I will remember that nothing I come to today is to be of regret. It simply is part of my path. What I learn from it is my gift.

October 22

Move Forward In Spite Of The Fear

Fear keeps me locked inside the miserable familiarity of dysfunction. When I stop myself from trying something new because it is unknown to me, I deny myself the opportunity of enjoyment. When I refuse to listen to new ideas because I'm so accustomed to doing things the same way over and over again, I halt my growth process. When I decide to stay within the confines of the childhood messages that swim through my mind, I am really deciding not to live.

It can be scary to try something new. It is often horrifying to walk into a room where I don't know one single person. The voice of my past tells me I will embarrass myself or look stupid if I do something other than what I've always done. Fortunately, I have learned that if I stay in the past, I never get to open the present. The future depends on my willingness to face my fears and move forward in spite of them.

Today: I will remember that no matter how scary the next new thing might be, it is my birthright to give it a try.

A Tragic Perspective

October 23

When it happens to me, it's a tragedy. Whether it is my car breaking down or my hair dryer dying when my hair is still wet, it's a tragedy. I'm especially annoyed when I find myself in a traffic jam or stuck in a long line at the bank. Why do these things always happen to me? Why am I the only one forced to deal with the tragedies of life?

Then I go home and turn on the television. I watch sitcom after sitcom and laugh my butt off as the characters get stuck in lines, lose power when they are trying to get ready for a big event, or find themselves late for an appointment by no fault of their own.

Why are the tragedies of my life so funny when they are happening to someone else? Maybe because they aren't really tragedies! Next time the line at the bank is five people deep, maybe I need to stop feeling sorry for myself because I have to wait, and remind myself that I'm blessed to have enough money to have a bank account at all.

Today: I will remember that breaking a fingernail is not a tragedy, even if I did just pay for a top-of-the-line manicure.

October 24

You Can't Win The Lottery If You Don't Buy A Ticket

There was a time when I was active in my addictions that I would sit on my bed and beg God to make me thin, give me the perfect man to fulfill my life, and make me sane and peaceful. And then I would continue to eat gluttonously, behave in unattractive and unprofessional ways, and drink myself into oblivion. I was waiting for God to change me, but I wasn't willing to do any of the work. Therefore, I remained imprisoned by my addictions.

It wasn't until I finally put down the fork, the beer bottle, and the men, and picked up the tools placed before me by those who had experience recovering from addiction, that God whisked me away from the obsessions and compulsions of my addictions.

His grace continues to surround me as long as I am willing to do my part to free myself.

Today: I will remember that God helps those who help themselves. What am I doing to help myself today?

Learning How I Don't Want To Be

October 25

I grew up with an alcoholic, egotistical father. There was nothing I wanted more than to be the exact opposite of him. Unfortunately I shared his addictive gene and for a good portion of my life, my behaviors were a precise reflection of his. While in my addictions, I denied any similarities I shared with him by continuing to use, and then just had to continue to deny by continuing to use, and so on. It was a vicious cycle.

As I have traveled the path of my recovery from addiction, I have recognized that certain behaviors of others often act as strong illustrations of how I don't want to be. When I am treated poorly by someone, or watch them as they look foolish while thinking they are being impressive, I file it away in my memory as unattractive and unwanted behavior for myself. And when something I do or say reminds me of my father, I quickly check my actions and motives and share my concerns with a trusted friend. I can then grow beyond my genes and toward God's will for me.

Today: I will remember that I can always learn from the behavior of others, even if it is simply a lesson in how I don't want to be.

OCTOBER 26

Messy Is Okay

My life isn't pretty. While I have worked diligently to "clean up the wreckage of my past" and continue to focus on bettering myself every day, I am still human and therefore can be pretty messy sometimes.

What I have learned over time is that messy is okay. I will never be perfect. I will always encounter situations that baffle me. I will often be hurt by things said or done by others. I will, in turn, cause those I love to feel pain, even if I don't intend to. This is all part of living, and it is okay.

When I forget that messy is okay, I find myself uncomfortable in my own skin. I begin looking to clear away the wreckage by numbing it with alcohol, food, or some other addictive substance. If I choose to look to God instead, He will remove the discomfort instead of numbing it to return at another time.

TODAY: I will remember that being messy is a part of being human and that only God can truly polish my heart and soul with comfort.

Looking For Gratitude

October 27

There was a five-year period in my life when I was working for a man who seemed to enjoy spreading misery. Every day it became more and more difficult to go into work until I realized that I was allowing this man's behavior to ruin my day. That was when I decided I would stop focusing on what he was doing and start focusing on the things about my job for which I was grateful. In addition, I drove into work each day and reminded myself that I only needed to work with him for this one day—and I can do anything for eight hours.

Amazingly, over time I became much more content at work and in my life. The gratitude I was making a point to recognize started to spill out into how I acted with others, and helped to free me from resentments that otherwise would have fermented inside of me. It was simply a matter of how I looked at my day, rather than what kind of day it was.

Today: I will remember that even in my darkest hour I can be grateful for something. I just need to be willing to look for it.

All Equal

Am I nicer to the hostess when in line at a crowded restaurant than I am to the valet who has already delivered my car from the parking lot? Is it my nature to smile and say hello to doctors in a hospital, while I just walk by a cleaning person without even acknowledging they are there? Do I see people as people or do I see them as class levels?

If I were to share honestly how I treat others, most often I would be embarrassed by my behavior. So many times I walk around thinking only of myself and asking, "What's in it for me?" This sort of attitude causes me to shun those who have less power and put on a pedestal those who have more. This short-sightedness and selfishness on my part leaves me feeling empty and fills me with shame. Is whatever the powerful person can do for me worth feeling this way?

Today: I will remember that everyone who crosses my path today is a human being who deserves to be treated with respect and kindness.

Fulfilled With God

For so long, I reached for things outside of myself to fill the void in my soul. Pizza, cheeseburgers, candy, beer, wine, cigarettes, men, shopping, and more—I thought that enough of these things would make me happy. The problem was that there was never enough of them to fill me up. I always longed for more. Even full to the edge of my throat on a binge of pizza and potato chips, I still craved a giant tub of ice cream. Even waking up with a hangover from too many vodka shots, I thought first of having a beer to take the edge off. And even when my heart was broken and shattered because of the callousness of some man, I still searched for the next boyfriend.

It's funny how denial so quickly turns into insanity—doing the same thing over and over and expecting different results. Food never filled me, but I kept on eating. Alcohol never removed the shame, but I kept on drinking. Men never comforted me, but I kept looking to them for comfort.

Now, after learning from my experiences and changing by embracing God's will for me with each step I take, I am fulfilled, satisfied, free, and joyous.

Today: I will remember that it is only through God's grace that I will find what I don't even know I am looking for.

Patience While Continuing To Act Equals Healing

When I have surgery, I want my body to bounce back right away. When I feel uncomfortable, I want that feeling to go away immediately. When I am struggling at work, I want to leave and find an easier job. When a relationship I am in is suffering through difficult times, I want it to improve as soon as possible.

Maybe this excessive need of mine to have things be okay instantly is part of the reason I was such a good addict. With a quick shot of alcohol, I could feel a little less uncomfortable and a little more like everything was okay. With a new man in my life, I could get caught up in the wonder of a new relationship and forget about my worries.

The problem with the addict's way of finding comfort is that the drink wears off and the new relationship eventually grows into a real-life saga. In order to find healing in any area of my life, I must continue to open my mind to God's will for me through new ideas, and follow the suggestions of those who have gone before me. I must learn to wait.

Today: I will remember to keep doing the next right thing while I'm waiting for healing to occur.

How I Act Speaks Volumes

October 31

If, when I came to a place in my life where I was ready to recover from my addictions, there was no one else in the world who had ever recovered, how would I have even been able to begin? It is through the strength, courage, and grace of others that I have been given the hope, faith, and inspiration I need to continue along the path of recovery each day.

It is only fair and just that I, in turn, carry an attractive message to others. If I am open-minded and responsible—new behaviors since I found recovery—I will encourage the same in others. If I am judgmental and rude, it makes it easier for those around me to behave similarly. What message do I carry today?

Today: I will remember that what Gandhi once said was absolutely true: "My life is my message."

Accepting My Humanness

Like most people, I have experienced times in my life when I felt hopeless, ashamed, and defeated. During those times, I have sometimes wallowed in self-pity, drank myself into oblivion, or binged on pizza and ice cream until I couldn't feel anything but stuffed like a Thanksgiving turkey. I was slowly committing suicide by drowning myself in the very shame that I wished didn't exist.

It has only been through the grace of God and the direction of some accepting and loving friends that I was able to find a way to swim to the edge of my shame, hopelessness, and defeat, and pull myself onto the shore of self-forgiveness and hope. What I realized during that process is this: I will always make mistakes, act out in ways for which I am not proud, and say things I wish I could take back. How I behave after I have done these things is what is most important to my continued growth in my relationship with God and others.

Today: I will remember that I am human and by nature, flawed. Marinating in my flaws gets me nowhere fast. Accepting them and working toward personal growth and change will keep my heart free and my soul at peace.

Loving Isn't Always Easy

November 2

My spouse may not be the person I want him to be today. He may be struggling with some of his own demons and spilling out resentments he has for others onto me. He may even be blaming me for hurts he feels from past relationships that have nothing to do with me.

Does this behavior of his give me the right to judge him or abandon him? Does it excuse me from loving and accepting him?

If I turn my back on my partner in his darkest hour, I do not know love.

I can accept him where he is today without allowing his darkness to become mine. I can love him for the thoughtful and wonderful man I know he is, instead of taking personally comments he may make that don't necessarily pertain to me or our relationship. He may be lost, but my love for him is not.

Today: I will remember that my husband and I will not always be in the same place emotionally. If I expect him to love me through my emotionally charged moments, shall I not offer him the same consideration?

NOVEMBER 3

Being Quiet With God

A suggestion made to me early in my recovery from addiction was to find a quiet time—try to make it the same time every day so it becomes a habit—and talk to God. If I don't feel comfortable talking to Him, I write Him a letter. And if I don't feel comfortable writing to Him, I just sit—maybe with my cat purring on my lap or while reading a daily meditation book like this one—and listen.

When I started doing this regularly, I felt better throughout each day. Eventually, it became something that I looked forward to before my feet even hit the floor in the morning. That was, and is, when it became a time when I was finally happy to see me.

TODAY: I will remember that taking time to be quiet with God each day helps me to grow into the person He has always wanted me to be—and that is when I begin to like who I am.

Cultivate New Ground

November 4

How long do I need to stay tangled in the weeds of my past and present grievances and resentments before I am ready to face the fear of plowing into the newness and uncertainty of learning, listening, and growing?

Will today be the day that I stand on a new foundation? Will I allow someone's words the room in my mind and heart to plant the seeds of hope and renewal I need to grow? Will I embrace the uncertainty by asking for help from another?

What will I choose to do today: cultivate the new ground or allow the weeds to grow?

Today: I will remember that untended weeds will overrun my life just as quickly as they do the beautiful landscaping outside my home.

NOVEMBER 5

Peace Isn't In A New Pair Of Shoes

My addictions only ever served to bring temporary satisfaction, as is true also for acquiring material things. I used to think that if I had a nicer car or a house on the beach, I'd be happy. But in the process of charging my way through department stores and online shopping websites, all I really had in the end was a credit card bill I couldn't afford and a whole lot of stuff that couldn't fill the hole in my soul any more than a pizza or a bottle of wine.

When I wake up in the morning and talk to God right away, asking Him to guide my steps, my words, my behaviors, and my heart—and then set out with faith in His guidance—that is when my soul is whole. Those are the days when peace comes to me, even when I can't afford to buy the new pair of snazzy boots I want. Those are the days when I can just be.

TODAY: I will remember that looking to things outside of myself to fulfill me will only end in heartache. As Dorothy Gale so succinctly put it, "If I ever go looking for my heart's desire again, I won't look any further than my own back yard."

Choose To See Light

November 6

Psychologists and learned men have lectured for hours on the simple idea that how a person perceives the world makes a huge difference in how he or she feels. Is the glass half empty or half full? I used to think that this line of thinking was a load of crap! If bad things happened to someone, how could they not feel bad?

Recently, while sitting in a meeting of friends sharing spiritual experiences, I heard a man say that the cancer he was diagnosed with six months ago was truly a blessing because it made him stop worrying about things that weren't important—like whether or not the weekend forecast of rain would keep him from playing golf—and start paying attention to the people in his life that he loves and the moments they share.

After hearing that, it became obvious to me that my perception of things is more than half the battle for living a happy and fulfilling life.

Today: I will remember that the long line at the bank can be an annoying inconvenience or a blessed opportunity to reflect on my day without rushing about. My perception of it—and ultimately my mood—is my choice.

NOVEMBER 7

Wanting To Be Well

Desperation was a gift for me, because it wasn't until I felt completely desperate that I began to want to do whatever I had to do to get well and recover from my addictive behaviors.

Up until that point, many people shared suggestions with me for losing weight, cutting down on my alcohol intake, finding a counselor who would help me overcome my childhood issues, etc. Most of them were very good suggestions from well-meaning people. But it didn't matter who said what to me back then. I still thought I had all the answers, would be able to find the right books to read, or could blame the sadness of my life on someone else. Before desperation, I may have needed help, but I didn't want it—and wanting to be well is the key to all recovery.

TODAY: I will remember that I can share my experiences, hope, and suggestions with others, but until they want to recover and grow, they won't.

I Hope

Looking to others to have my expectations fulfilled is dangerous. Only I can know what I truly want and need. If I look to another with the expectation that he will read my mind and comfort me whenever I'm in need of comfort, or send me flowers whenever I need to be cheered up, I will be disappointed. And that disappointment will eventually lead me to become resentful that he doesn't love me enough, or the right way.

Instead of expecting life to be a certain way, or expecting my mate to send me a bouquet of flowers on a special anniversary, I now choose to be hopeful. I hope my life will be peaceful and fulfilling. I hope to be appreciated and loved by others. I hope to always be willing to carry out God's will for me. Just for today, I hope.

TODAY: I will remember that I can have hope without expectations getting in the way and causing me to become resentful. All I have to do is continue to ask God for guidance and do my best to follow His path for me. When I am honestly adhering to that simple principle, I can never be disappointed.

November 9

There Is No One Right Way To Meditate

Going for a walk and appreciating the trees, flowers, and autumn aroma that wafts through the air. Sitting on the couch with my cat on my lap and stroking her coat as she purrs a tune of God's whispering love. Listening to the sounds of ocean waves and seagulls chirping about as I feel the warmth of the sun on my face on a summer afternoon. Relaxing in a bubble bath by candlelight.

Meditation does not have to be an officially guided tour of yoga positions or "Oms" and clanging cymbals. Meditation is whatever draws me closer to God's private message for me.

Today: I will remember that I can meditate anywhere, anytime. All I need to do is stop and listen.

God's Goodness Is Never Difficult

It's not always easy to do or say the "right" thing. Sure, there is the occasional "pay it forward" movie theme or commercial on television, but for the most part the world is filled with self-centered people trying to get what they want, when they want it. We all get in each other's way, and that can make being kind to one another very difficult.

It is only through my relationship with God that I will be taken beyond any difficulty of being good and toward the light of helping another and the peace of self-care. Through His grace, I am given the opportunities and the dignity I need to carry His goodness to my fellows. In that, the possibilities of goodness are endless.

Today: I will remember that it is when I am relying only on myself and my humanness that being good is difficult.

NOVEMBER 11

Climb Out Of The Tomb Of Self

It takes a daily regime of self-searching and admitting my faults to continue to grow and change into the person God has planned for me to be. Sometimes I can feel overwhelmed by looking within and "doing the next right thing" all the time. If I give in to that overwhelmed feeling, I become stuck in a place of self-pity and apathy. When I remain stuck there for too long, my growth is halted and my inner peace slowly begins to corrode.

The emptiness I feel during these times is a warning signal that my self-centeredness is interrupting my relationship with God. I can accept this warning gratefully and use it to climb out of the tomb of self and into the love of God. My energies and enthusiasm will be revived the moment I look to Him for comfort.

TODAY: I will remember that I will continue to experience love in my life only if I take the daily steps needed to grow in my relationship with God.

God Is Not A Building

NOVEMBER 12

My dad was a minister. Growing up, I went to church every Sunday, every holiday, and every summer for vacation Bible school. I learned a lot about the stories in the Bible and I came to believe that there was a God. The problem for me was that I never really felt what I learned. Going to church and learning all the proper lessons only gave me a place to visit and things to read about. When I left the church in my early twenties, I was full of fear, not faith.

Today I meet up with God in convenience stores, my dining room, lines at the grocery store, and when visiting with friends. He guides my steps and my behaviors when I ask Him to, and He gives me strength and courage when I most need them. Because I seek His truth regularly, I don't feel any closer to Him when I'm in a church than when I'm sitting in my car in a traffic jam.

TODAY: I will remember that my relationship with God is not about a place or a religion. It is about my desire to follow His will, instead of my own.

November 13

Self-Pity Is Deception

Oh, woe is me! If only everyone knew how difficult my life is, they would be nicer to me. When will I ever catch a break?

This type of self-pity served as a comforting massage to my ego for a very long period in my life. I would often soothe my fears and disappointments with a plethora of similarly self-indulgent thoughts of deception.

For that is exactly what self-pity is: deception. It is my disease of self-centeredness and selfishness that wants me to believe the lie that I am the only person who has ever experienced difficult moments. It wants me to ignore the fact that everyone who walks the earth faces tough times and hardships. It wants me to turn away from others and into myself.

But that lonely state it takes me to is what finally brings me to reality. Being human, it is unnatural to be without the love and companionship of others. And that is when I recognize the lie and discomfort of my self-pity. Once I am aware of it, I can take a step away from it by calling a friend, saying a prayer, asking for help, or writing a gratitude list. Even in the midst of difficult times, I can always find gratitude.

Today: I will remember to be thankful today, no matter what is going on in my life.

Communicate With Respect

November 14

I used to think that standing up for myself meant being a bitch and telling people off. Needless to say, this type of communication never helped me build strong and healthy relationships with others.

Since finding my way to recovery from my addictions, I've been given new tools for living. Through those tools, I've learned that taking care of my own needs and being clear about what I need from others can actually be done in peaceful and respectful ways. I can be straight-forward without yelling. I can ask for what I need without being selfish. I can be open and honest about my feelings without blaming anyone for them. I can take responsibility for my actions without making excuses. And I can keep from saying things that might hurt others by filtering my thoughts before blurting out everything that runs through my mind.

Today: I will remember that taking care of myself does not mean that I must ignore the feelings and needs of others.

NOVEMBER 15

Hope And Continue To Live In Reality

I used to go to a fantastical place to escape reality, where I dreamed about the things I wanted. I imagined giving my acceptance speech after receiving an Oscar—though I'm not an actor— or singing the national anthem after winning an Olympic gold medal in gymnastics—though I've never even practiced tumbling—or being carried out of the factory by "an officer and a gentleman"—though I weighed over 250 pounds. The dreams were outrageously impossible.

There is nothing wrong with dreaming; it's the absurd fantasies that got me nowhere. When I dream reasonable dreams, I give myself permission to hope. That hope provides the energy and enthusiasm I need to continue working toward fulfilling my dreams. Balanced with a firm foothold in reality, I can trust my life's path, no matter where it may lead.

TODAY: I will remember that a balance of hope and reality will keep me focused on God's will, while allowing my soul to fly.

The Beauty Of The Struggle

November 16

Looking back at history, I see slaves fighting to be free men. I see women struggling to be recognized as equals. I see people fleeing countries to create their own free state of living. These paths to freedom often led to suffering, illness, abuse, and death. But through these struggles, determination and faith prevailed and people were able to reach their desired "mountaintop" of freedom.

Equally so, achieving freedom from addiction is a battle. The journey through recovery is never an easy one. Yes, there are peaks of happiness along the way, but the dark, deep valleys of struggle will always be a part of the process. The beauty of the struggle lies in what is offered to all those who are willing to accept the truth of their addiction. Once I admit that I am powerless over my addiction, I can embrace the experience, strength, and hope of all those who have walked the path before me. With that, I recognize that I am no longer alone in my valleys, or in my happiness.

Today: I will remember that to grow, I must struggle. So for today, I will be grateful for the difficult moments that are part of the process of living.

November 17

Stepping Outside Of Myself

Sometimes I don't want to smile and say hello to the cashier at the supermarket. Sometimes I feel like ignoring the needs of others and only doing what I want to do. Sometimes I just don't care about anyone but myself. Sometimes I can be really selfish.

Being thoughtful of the needs of others isn't always the easiest thing to do—or what I want to do, for that matter. But I have found that it is during those times when I reach outside of myself and follow God's will, that I am blessed with a message I never could have seen or accepted in the "safety" and "comfort" of my own selfishness.

Today: I will remember that being selfish builds a wall between me and true fulfillment: knowing and doing God's will.

Choosing To Be Happy Today

November 18

I can try to control what's going on around me, or I can accept life as it comes and do my best with what is presented to me. I can worry about what medical tests will reveal, or trust that my body will continue to exist as long as I'm needed to carry God's message. I can wait to be happy until I have enough money, enough love, enough free time, and enough stuff, or I can be grateful for the blessings in my life today. It is always my choice.

Today: I will remember that living in tomorrow will only serve to rob me of the joys of today.

November 19

Finding Humor In My Humanness

If I'm not paying attention to where I'm walking and I trip over a bump in the sidewalk, I laugh. It's funny when I do something silly or trip over my own two feet. So why do I have such a hard time finding humor when I revert to old behaviors and say something I wish I hadn't, or act in a way that isn't quite that dignified?

If only I could grasp the concept of humility, which tells me I am exactly where God wants me to be for today. I may say silly things or act immature when I don't get my way, but that doesn't make me a bad person. In fact, if I can look at those actions and find a way to find humor in my humanness, I may even be able to learn from it.

Today: I will remember that being human is funny.

Open-Mindedness

When I was in college, I was a hippie chick, lazily getting drunk and high and pontificating the troubles of society. I thought my ideas for bettering the world were the only ones that would make a difference.

As I have grown older, my mind has slowly opened to the suggestions of others. I have recognized the need to loosen my grip on the opinions I once so fiercely held. I can move beyond my ego and accept that someone else's belief may make sense if I am willing to open my mind and soul to its energy.

I am grateful today that I have stopped blocking out alternate points of view and anyone who might disagree with me. With each new thought or differing opinion that I welcome into my heart, I grow just a little bit more into the person God wants me to be.

TODAY: I will remember that a new idea embraced—rather than feared—is a graceful move forward.

November 21

You Can't Please Everyone All The Time

I once heard someone say, "What other people think of me is none of my business." At that point in my life, I spent so much time worrying if people liked me or not that it never dawned on me it didn't really matter. Not only did I worry about what others thought, I also spent a lot of time trying to do things to get others to like me and think I was a good person.

While I was spending all this time people-pleasing, I was ignoring my own needs and wishes and subconsciously thinking less and less of myself. Discovering that what others thought of me wasn't a crucial part of my growth process led me to the fact of life that what I thought of me was the most important stepping stone to finding self-respect.

Over time, I realized that no matter what I do or say, I won't be able to make everyone happy all the time. In fact, there will be people in this world who do not like me. That's just reality. The key to self-respect within that reality is to like myself, even in their presence.

Today: I will remember that if people don't respect or appreciate me, that is their prerogative. The only me I can be is the one that I respect and appreciate.

Letting Go Brings Peace

November 22

When I walked through the doors of recovery from addiction, I was told I had to give up control of my life and ask for help. Some people find this concept impossible, but I found it to be a huge relief. While I spent my days in active addiction pretending to be in control, I always knew—deep down inside—that I had absolutely no control of my life. Admitting my powerlessness over my addictions was an absolute blessing!

Taking the next step by turning my entire life over to a power greater than myself was when the smashing of my ego, pride, and fear began. I no longer could follow my addictive urges—in regards to food and alcohol, but also in regards to relationships, family matters, shopping, etc. I had to look at the consequences of my actions before I carried them out. I had to learn to take responsibility for things I did and said. I had to grow up and let go of any control I thought I had over others. I had to accept that I am powerless over people and events, just as much as I am powerless over my addictions.

I never would have believed that letting go of control of all these things would bring peace to my heart and soul, but it has only been through trusting God's path and following it that I have become truly free.

Today: I will remember that when I have the urge to control a person or situation, I am inviting disease to block my view of God's plan for me. This is exactly when I need to let go and ask for help.

November 23 Actions And Reactions

Because of my ego, I have often been goaded into engaging in dangerous communications with someone who is living in an active addiction or co-dependency. There is something deep down inside of me that knows nothing I say will be heard by an active addict, but there is also a part of me that doesn't want anyone to think they have quieted me with their anger. In these instances, I have discovered that in reacting to the other person's unhealthy behaviors, I have given the disease exactly what it wants: confrontation and continued dysfunction.

I must remember that how a person treats me reflects their true nature, and how I react to that treatment reflects mine. I can't change how others behave or what they say to me, but I can respond with dignity and grace, even in the darkest of circumstances. This takes an awful lot of practice and isn't always easy, but it is always worth walking away with my self-respect intact.

Today: I will remember to pause before I react to others. In that moment of quiet, I can wait for guidance from God and carry out His will instead of feeding the disease of dysfunction.

G.O.D.—Good Orderly Direction

For so long I blamed all my problems on my parents and how they raised me. You would be as miserable as I was if you grew up in a dysfunctional family like mine. I suppose it was easier to deny how much I disliked myself if it was someone else's fault. I could go on believing that I was a victim and was to be pitied.

The problem with pity was that it didn't provide me with inner peace and self-respect. Eventually the pity from others disappeared and I was left with myself—alone, depressed, and hopeless. At this point, there was no one left to blame and I had to recognize my true enemy in the mirror. In that recognition I found a path to my soul, where I could glide away from my fears and into faith. All I had to do was exchange who I was and where I wasn't going for the healthy me who wanted to live.

TODAY: I will remember that when I am willing to get out of my own way and follow good orderly direction from others, I am experiencing a miracle.

Take One Step

One of my favorite songs from childhood is "Put One Foot in Front of the Other," which was sung in the television special Santa Claus is Comin' to Town. The song was planted in a scene where one character was trying to encourage another character, who felt lost and alone, to just keep moving—to keep trying. I sang this song over and over again to myself when I was a kid. In fact, to this day I remember it when I'm feeling defeated.

It isn't always easy to "keep on keeping on." Some days I just want to run home and get back in bed. It seems easier to think of stopping the rotation of the earth by hiding under the covers than to continue on through a dreary day of difficult moments. But if I can remember the lyrics to this childhood song, I know this: "If you want to change your direction; If your time of life is at hand; Well, don't be the rule, be the exception; A good way to start is too stand."

TODAY: I will remember that no matter how difficult a situation may seem, I only need to keep putting one foot in front of the other to get through it.

Puncture My Ego, Please!

NOVEMBER 26

There's nothing worse than an injured ego. The feeling is intensely personal and internally disturbing. As it is happening, it is difficult to recognize the benefit. Yet in looking back over my life and experiences, I see the most significant changes have occurred only after I have been broken down from the egotistical me into a moldable form of humanness. In fact, without some of the moments of utter humiliation that I have experienced, I may never have become desperate enough to give up on everything I thought I knew and ask for help.

TODAY: I will remember that when my ego feels punctured, it may just be time for another blessing of growth to occur.

A Channel Of God

"Now go; I will help you speak and teach you what to say."
Exodus 4:12, New International Version

So often during life's difficult situations, I find myself without the perfect words to share with a friend in need, a relative suffering from an illness, or a co-worker who is frustrated with his or her job. I want to utter the most profound statement that will catapult someone into an area of faith that will carry them to serenity. Instead, I say something stupid—or that sounds stupid to me.

What I need to remember is that even Moses feared speaking to others. He had the Ten Commandments in his hands and still questioned if he would be able to carry God's message in a way that others would understand. God's words to him were simple: to just go and do as He had instructed, and He would give Moses the words.

Today: I will remember that God will speak through me if I am willing to continue to follow His path for me.

Keep Your Eyes Focused On The Path In Front Of You

How much of my time is spent worrying about what other people are doing or saying? How often do I point out the defects of my family members? When was the last time I reminded someone else of a task they needed to complete at work?

All of this attention I pay to the behaviors of those around me is pointless. I have absolutely no control over whether or not someone else tries to improve their life. I can't make someone finish a project on time by pointing out their procrastination. My comments to family members about how I think they need to change only provides opportunity for resentment.

The only thing I have any control over is how I follow my own path. And when I'm busy watching how others are walking, I'm sure to veer off course.

Today: I will remember to keep my judging eyes on myself.

November 29

Procrastination Is A Sign To Take Action

When I was in college, I was all about leaving my studies go until the day before—or hour before—the final exam. It made for a whole lot of fun throughout the semester—one day of extreme panic, and then long-lasting and overwhelming regret. Sadly, I didn't learn to change this type of procrastinating behavior until long after I graduated—by the skin of my teeth.

What I have learned since those irresponsible days of my youth is that when I don't feel like doing something, it is a sign that I must do it. Whether it is a project at work, reading a meditation book, or tackling a pile of yet-to-be addressed Christmas cards, letting it go will only weigh heavily on my peace of mind.

Today: I will remember that when I start pushing off until tomorrow what I can do today, I am setting myself up for internal uneasiness.

Self-Honesty Is Freedom

November 30

I used to tell myself I didn't have a problem with alcohol because I never drove drunk. Then, after I graduated to taking the risk of driving while intoxicated, I told myself that I didn't have a problem because I only did it when it was absolutely necessary. I also spent my entire life knowing that I had a problem with food, but always telling myself that the next diet would be the one that fixed my problem. The fact that I was addicted to both alcohol and food made it easier for me to believe these lies. The longer I believed my own lies, the longer I could stay comfortable in my active addictions.

For some addicts, the moment of recognition of the addiction never arrives. For others, it enters suddenly and whisks the addict up into a land of rebirth and glory. But for most, it gradually descends and slowly wraps itself around the ego, cushioning it for the fall to the bottom, where we finally see the truth: that we are powerless over that substance or behavior and the only answer is complete abstinence from it.

Today: I will remember that recovery from any addiction is about being honest—most importantly with myself.

Being The Real Me

I tried for a long time to be something I wasn't. I did whatever it took to please others, no matter how bad it made me feel about myself. I pretended to understand things that confused me and to act in ways that felt uncomfortable in order to make myself look normal. I wanted everyone around me to think I had all the answers and knew exactly what I wanted out of life.

My attempt at being someone other than who I really was, was my way of trying to walk out of my own story. Some people try the geographical cure by moving to a new town and trying to start over. Either way, we always bring our real selves along—whether we are pretending to be someone else, or running from the people who know who we really are.

Once I accepted that my story involved recovering from addiction and lifelong dysfunction, I could stop running away from it.

TODAY: I will remember that I don't need to try to be someone I'm not or avoid the path before me out of fear. Who I am and the path I travel are mine.

People Change And Grow; Love Changes And Grows

When I first fell in love with my husband, my heart would leap whenever I saw him or heard his voice. The excitement of how much he cared about me traveled through me like lightning whenever I thought about us together. I couldn't wait to be with him.

As our relationship has shifted and changed over time, I have discovered feelings of love that go far beyond those initial days of "puppy" love and excitement. For the first time in my life, I have experienced the desire to feel pain for someone so that they don't have to feel it. And I have also experienced loving a person, but not liking them very much.

What has continually been brought to my attention throughout this process is the fact that as long as he and I are both growing and learning as individuals, our love will also change and grow with each passing day.

TODAY: I will remember to express my love to my husband, and to accept wherever we are in our journey together at each moment.

Serving Selflessly

No matter what I'm doing or where I am—at work, on vacation, taking a walk, visiting with friends, writing a story, or spending time with my family—if I'm thinking only about what I'm going to get out of it, I'm missing the point. My best bet for finding inner peace is in how I serve my higher power and those around me. Instead of asking myself, "What do I want to get out of this?" I must ask, "How can I serve God in my work?" or, "What can I do to make this situation easier for the people around me?"

The point is not to be a doormat or slave to others, but to remember that when I step outside of my self-seeking and selfish behaviors, I move closer to God. When I simplify my motives into bringing joy and comfort, I receive more peace than I ever could have imagined.

TODAY: I will remember that too often people ignore the needs of others while striving for what they want. Today I will pay attention to the needs of others before stepping over them to get what I want.

Awareness, Acceptance, And Action

December 4

Am I expressing my anger through lashing out at others? Am I pushing my rage down by eating to excess or holding resentments in a frozen scowl? Am I even aware that I am angry?

When I deny that I sometimes act out in defective ways, I harm myself and others. It is important for me to recognize how and when I am behaving in these unhealthy ways and talk to someone about it. Once I have spoken to a trusted friend or advisor, I can let go of the shame that I once carried and embrace my newfound ability to accept myself as I am. In that acceptance, I can remove the cloak of my shortcomings—whether it be the look on my face, the way I talk to others, or the wall of fat that I wear to protect myself from harm—and begin to display an image of peace instead.

Today: I will remember that when I am uncomfortable with the way I am acting or feeling, I need to talk to a friend about it.

December 5

Positive Thoughts Breed Positive Changes

As long as I am stuck on the hamster wheel in my mind, running over and over all the horrible things people have done to me and the bad breaks the world has served me, I will never be able to truly enjoy the gift of life. In order for my soul to be able to live a life free of resentment, self-righteous judgment, and the like, I must be willing to steer away from negative thinking. I need to ask for help, first from my higher power and then from others who share my afflictions.

Once I have started to replace negative thoughts with healthier, more encouraging principles, my mind will begin to open to new ideas for living a better life, one day at a time. I will become lighter, moment by moment. I will welcome joy instead of harboring sadness. I will begin to trust, rather than doubt.

This personal development and newborn willingness may soon be criticized by those in this world who choose to stay stuck. How I care for myself in the midst of such disparagement will be a true test of my willingness and faith.

Today: I will remember that with each positive thought, I unlock another latch on the door to happiness. How others perceive me as I change my way of thinking is none of my business.

I Get What I Give

December 6

When I was a kid, I walked around with open hands, assuming the world would always give me what I wanted. The first time my mother suggested I try to find a summer job I was a teenager and highly offended that she would expect me to start earning my own pocket money. I begrudgingly took a position serving snacks on a golf course, and did only the bare minimum necessary to get by.

I work at a college now and I envy the work ethic I see in some of the students who have to pay their own way through school. Some of them have two or three part-time jobs to pay for their tuition. They work hard and study hard. They appreciate the education they are receiving. I see them believing in themselves more and more with each day and each semester. Their struggles to make ends meet and their willingness to do whatever they must to improve themselves are helping them to see the value in it all. They are learning at a young age what it took me almost forty years to grasp: I get what I give.

Today: I will remember that hard work and dedicated enthusiasm will always come back to me—maybe not today or tomorrow, but someday.

I Am Funny

As I was putting my seven-foot artificial Christmas tree together this year, I noticed a mistake when I was almost halfway finished: I had put the bottom piece on third. My first thought was to belittle myself and curse the fact that I had to take it apart and start over. But then I looked at it again and saw how absolutely silly it looked. I got quite a chuckle out of my mistake and actually thought—just for a split second—about how funny it would be if I left it that way.

There is something wonderful about being able to laugh at myself. It is a true acceptance of my humanness. When I am able to accept myself as I truly am, not only can I watch with a sense of humor as I sometimes stumble through life, I can also appreciate my grace in times of struggle and my dignity in the face of confrontation.

TODAY: I will remember to appreciate every part of who I am—the silly, the confident, the uncertain and the courageous.

I Am One Seed

I spend an awful lot of time trying to figure out what my purpose is here on earth. I ponder and I think and I talk about it with friends. I write and I cry and I struggle to know for certain what I am supposed to be doing. I have inklings of intuition, but when I grasp for them they quickly disappear into the unidentified future of my journey. The inklings are like seeds in an apple. I see them and I can count them, but what do they mean?

In God's world, I am just one of those seeds. I am planted and set to grow. I don't know what will sprout from my limbs or what pollen I may produce to float on the stream of consciousness around me. All I know is that as long as I am planted firmly in the healthy soil of God's path, I will grow and produce as He has planned. I can't produce without Him. I can't grow alone. I can only rest in today's soil in preparation for the sunlight of tomorrow that will guide me to bud and ripen.

Today: I will remember that trying to figure out my purpose will only push me farther away from it. When I relax near God, I will be more likely to hear His voice and follow it.

December 9

If It Is Unknown, It Can't Be Changed

True terror lies in identifying that which is evil about me. Could I possibly have inside me the makings of something horrible? Something unspeakable? Could I possess the ability to harm with intent?

The answer is simple: yes.

It is in that clear positive answer that I find the courage to fight the evil inside. Once I have recognized and identified the potential insidiousness of my diseased character, I can begin to overcome it.

Today: I will remember that the unknown parts of me are those that are impossible to change. With each moment of self-searching and honest appraisal, I can find every character defect that separates me from God and begin to amend it.

I Am The Fault Of No One

I used to blame everything on my father because he was an alcoholic. Then, after some therapy in my late teens and early twenties, I transferred the blame to my mother because she stayed with him instead of leaving and protecting her children from his rage and dysfunction. I could've done so much more with my life if someone had just told me I had potential. I could've been someone.

I've found that it is only when I am willing to look honestly at myself and take responsibility for my actions that I am able to forgive those who have harmed me along the way. And in order to embrace a true sense of self-respect, I also need to forgive myself for years of denying I ever had a part in my troubles.

As a grown woman, I now know that even though I didn't receive support for my passions as I was growing up, I still have the opportunity to be anything I want to be.

Today: I will remember that I have choices today and if I don't go for what I want, I have only myself to blame.

December 11

There Is Always A Solution

I've never been very good at accepting criticism. Even when someone is constructive in their analysis of how I do something in an effort to help me, I still don't receive it well. Of course, I have never been one to hold back on correcting others when they make a mistake. I suppose, in an effort to make myself look better, I lean toward judging and condemning others.

As I have strengthened my spirit through daily communion with God, I have recognized that in addition to the discomfort I feel when I receive criticism, I also feel a certain unease settle into my soul when I give it to others or to myself. To change my direction away from this path of dis-ease, I can work to offer a solution instead of pointing out a mistake, or recognize the good in a mishap rather than focusing on the trouble it has caused.

Today: I will remember to look at a problem, a mistake, or a crisis from all angles before I begin to complain about its presence.

Showing Up Is Only Part Of The Process

"Showing up" means more than just going to church every Sunday. In fact, I believe that to God, showing up isn't necessarily about going to church regularly. For me, showing up means communicating with God every day.

I also believe that God doesn't really care how, when, or where I communicate with Him, as long as I communicate with Him. I can talk to Him silently in my mind or out loud on my knees beside my bed. I can sing to Him and show Him my gratitude by appreciating the natural world around me. I can write letters to Him to express my dissatisfaction with the way things are in my life, or to share with Him my desires. I can even yell at Him when I'm angry. I have done this and have not yet been struck down by lightning!

As long as I'm honest and as long as I'm willing to watch and listen for His response, God doesn't care how I communicate with Him!

TODAY: I will remember to open my heart and soul to God through honest communication.

More Is Never Enough

Most of my life has been swallowed up by the need for more. No matter how much I had of something, I wanted more. No matter how much weight I lost, I never hit my goal. No matter what job I was getting paid to do, it wasn't my dream.

After many years of self-searching, I have discovered the truth in finding enough. I'm currently not working in my dream job, but for today it's enough. I wouldn't be heartbroken if the bathroom scale told me I weighed five pounds less than I do, but for today my body size is good enough. I still live paycheck to paycheck, but I have all that I need.

The only difference in my life today is that I have found self-respect and self-acceptance through my relationship with God. Trusting that He has a plan for me allows everything in my life today to be enough. For it is everything in my life today that is leading to His ultimate design.

TODAY: I will remember that when I think I need more of something, I need to stop and ask myself if it is my desire or God's plan that guides me.

I Am Not Equipped To Be A Label Maker

December 14

My first instinct when I see a person—especially a stranger that I walk past on the street—is to label them. Right away they are "important" because they are wearing a suit, or "irresponsible" because they have an eyebrow piercing.

If I take my judgments one step further, I can even recognize that I continue to label a person even after I've met them. They become "annoying" or "funny" or "boring."

Is it ever possible to know enough about a person to assign a label to them? I don't believe it is. Just because someone dresses a certain way or expresses themselves in a manner that offends me does not mean I can understand who they are. Furthermore, how would I feel if someone labeled me?

Today: I will remember that when I label someone, I put up a wall in my mind and heart to learning about who they really are.

December 15

I Rarely Know What I Need To Be Happy

What I wished to be when I grew up is not what I believe would fulfill me today—I doubt I could handle the celebrity of being named Miss America. And today, I may wish to sit and write all day long. However, because I am not independently wealthy, I will instead go to work and do the job for which I receive a paycheck.

What comes next on my path is not necessarily my choice. But because it is my path, it is my responsibility to face it, walk through it with as much dignity and grace as possible, and learn from it.

Today: I will remember that what I think I want is rarely what ends up giving me inner peace and contentment.

There Is No Age Limit On A Dream

December 16

For most of my life I listened to the messages that told me I wasn't good enough, so I didn't even try. Since I've come to the realization that I am good enough and that what I have to offer is worthy, I find myself feeling more challenged by the message that says I'm too old to start something new.

Just because I turn twenty-five, or thirty, or forty—oh no!—doesn't mean I have to give up my dreams and settle for the way life is. Laura Ingalls Wilder didn't have her first book published until she was sixty-five years old. I recently watched a friend complete her college education—it took her over a decade of night classes—and she's now beginning her dream job at the age of fifty. If they can keep after their dreams at fifty and sixty-five, what's stopping me?

Today: I will remember that even though I'm not living in my dreams at the age of forty-one, doesn't mean I'm too old to still be chasing them.

DECEMBER 17

God Is My Shield

Evilness is real. If I pretend it doesn't exist, I am in denial. If I think I can protect myself from it, I am mistaken.

It is only through my relationship with God that I am shielded from the evil that lurks among us. I cannot recognize it or defend against it if I am not in daily communication with Him. I cannot turn away from it if I am fighting its tempting promises with my own power. And if I choose to walk alone in the presence of evil, I will be swallowed up into the belly of the beast.

God is my refuge. God is my strength and my armor. God is the only guaranteed buffer between me and evil.

TODAY: I will remember to ask God for protection from all evil.

Take A Breath

December 18

Ethel Merman, the great Broadway star, once said, "I take a breath when I have to." It seems like such a simple statement. Just take a breath when you need to. But how often do I forget this important part of life?

Rushing from here to there and everywhere, trying to get everything done on time and make everyone else happy leaves little room for feeding my own soul with the breath of my higher power.

Ethel Merman had one of the most powerful voices to ever grace the stage of show business. There was no "learning" to breathe for her. When she needed to breathe, she took a breath. Perhaps I was never meant to have to learn to breathe. Perhaps I am just meant to take a breath when I have to.

Today: I will remember to breathe in the spirit of life.

December 19

Negativity Spreads

Negativity spreads far and wide and at a quick pace. I've been at sporting events where a team is playing poorly, and by halftime fans that were spouting praises in the parking lot are now booing at the players and calling for the coach's resignation. At times, I've joined in with a boo or a hiss myself. It's easy to do when the guy next to me is doing the same thing.

Sadly life often imitates this model of behavior. If one person in the office has a problem with the boss, after a few days of complaining and stating their case, several others are on board supporting the problem—with only one half of the story under their belts. For some reason, we all feel better about a negative feeling if others feel it also. But is that a good enough excuse for planting negativity wherever I go?

Today: I will remember to keep my negative feelings to myself until I can speak to a trusted friend or advisor about them. I am in no position to taint the thoughts of others when I am feeling less than positive.

People Who Care Have Good Manners

December 20

To barrel through life like a bull in a china shop is simply rude. It illustrates an attitude of self-centeredness—an unwillingness to care about others.

My experience has shown me that when I express interest in the worries, cares, joys, and triumphs of my friends and family, I am giving value to their journey. And when I am asked for feedback and I am willing to share my insights, I am establishing unity and giving strength to everyone involved.

What another person cares about might not matter much to me. What's important is that the person matters to me.

Today: I will remember that in recognizing and respecting the feelings of the people around me, I am providing a wonderful service to mankind.

December 21

This Moment Is What Counts

Be centered in today.
Stay in the moment.
Think not of where you will be or how you will feel when it is over.
Recognize the beauty of a raindrop.
Appreciate the air you breathe.
Feel the love in the smile of a friend.
Enjoy the ride, bumpy as it may sometimes be.
Ask for nothing; accept it all.

Today: I will remember that staying within the present moment in my mind, my heart, and my soul allows me to be fully aware of what my higher power is offering.

Sanity Is Wonderful

DECEMBER 22

For me, active addiction was insanity. Within it, there were moments of absolute sanity—or awakening—when I was given the opportunity to follow the light or stay in the darkness. With the exception of one time—the last time—whenever I was presented with that absolute sanity, it horrified me and I turned and ran back into the hell of eating, drinking, men, money, or whatever the flavor of the moment was.

Most gratefully, I look upon that last time when the sanity—the awakening—occurred and I wrapped my arms and legs and heart and soul around it. Whatever was needed to stay connected to it, I was committed to doing it. However I had to change to live in it, I was willing. And I still am.

TODAY: I will remember that the possibility of turning back to the insanity will always remain within me. But the beauty of this interval of sanity that is called recovery is that, rather than horrible, it is wonderful.

December 23

Truth Is The Salve That Saves

The truth is powerful. Yet it cannot be forced upon someone who is not ready to hear it. My own experience has shown me that even when I most needed to hear it, the truth was lost on me until my heart was open to receive it. This is so because denial is also powerful.

But when denial is lifted, even just by a minute amount, the truth has the ability to blindly go where no lie could ever have reached deep within my soul. This is the moment when the truth begins to heal. It heals the wounds that have been rubbed raw through the process of self-discovery, as well as those that have become infected by continual exposure to dysfunction and disease.

Simply put, truth is the salve that saves.

Today: I will remember that to be honest with myself and with others, while remaining respectful, is one of the greatest gifts I can offer.

Pray For Those Who Disturb You

DECEMBER 24

Most of the time, my dad was drunk and loud and extremely embarrassing. I was always bothered by his constant need to act in inappropriate ways in public. I never thought that these antics were his way of trying to get someone to help him. Even if it was subconsciously motivated, he was yelling out for someone to notice and soothe his pain. I just thought he was being a drunk, insulting jerk.

Today, as I come in contact with others who are acting obnoxiously, I try to remind myself that their behavior is coming from a place of loneliness and fear that I may know nothing about. I must ask myself, "Who am I to judge this person?"

This doesn't mean I have to accept every attitude of perversion or every mean comment directed my way. It doesn't mean I have to pretend to like everyone and laugh at jokes I find offensive. But it does mean that when I am disturbed by someone's behavior, I need to allow for the possibility that deep down inside that person may be suffering and in need of my prayers instead of my judgment.

TODAY: I will remember to say a prayer for those who disturb my serenity.

Striving For Peace

"What good will it be for a man if he gains the whole world, yet forfeits his soul?"

Matthew 16:26, New International Version

Do I need to be in control of everything to feel better about myself? What am I willing to do and say to have power over others? Must I hold a title of superiority at work to feel complete? Is my mission in life to be richer and more popular than anyone I know?

When I am trying to control, I am actually out of control. When I am lying and scheming in order to get my way, I have lost all the strength that comes with a peaceful soul. When I step on others to gain more money, more fame, or more accolades, I am alone and cut off from the spirit of life.

If God's will for me is a successful life, then that success will come with peace and a full heart.

TODAY: I will remember that all the money, fame, and praise in the world can't come close to fulfilling me as does the inner peace that comes from trying to know and carry out God's will each day.

We Will Always Be Human

December 26

Recently my husband was snippy with me while he was trying to work on finances. I was simply asking about his interest in a social invitation we had received, and he remarked nastily that he didn't care. I felt dismissed and unimportant. I walked away deflated and hurt.

A little while later, my husband came to me, hugged me, and said he was sorry. He acknowledged his harsh tone and told me there was no excuse for his behavior. The bratty little child inside of me wanted to stay mad—"How dare he treat me that way?" But the grown-up woman was reminded of the fact that at some point in the future, I would probably say or do something for which I would desire his forgiveness. I am, after all, human too.

So instead of pouting and turning away from him, I hugged him back and told him I understood and appreciated his apology.

Today: I will remember that my husband is making his way through life and our relationship exactly as I am: one mistake, one triumph, and one precious moment at a time.

Accepting Myself

When I look to others for approval, there is something within my soul that I need to confront, accept, and move beyond. For when I am looking to someone else to tell me I am okay or to make me feel better about myself, I am obviously not at peace. And it is only for a few moments after someone praises me that I feel good about myself. Not long after the accolades, I slide back into whatever discomfort or insecurity that was already at play.

The permanence of feeling good about myself has only come to me as I have learned to accept all of my humanness—good and bad qualities, defects, and talents, alike. It is something that I need to re-learn and review often, mainly because I have a built in "forgetter" that attempts to lure me back to messages from my past that tell me I need to belittle myself. Like everything else in life, my acceptance of who I am is a one-day-at-a-time journey.

Today: I will remember to be as kind and gentle with myself as I would to a close friend in need.

Don't Run Away—Change

December 28

I wish I could just run away! How many times have we all thought or said that? If only that could solve all our problems, we'd all have our bags packed and be on our way to happiness.

It is true that when I am bothered by something in my life, it is usually because of something within me that is off-kilter. The good news is that if there is anything I can change in this world, it is me! Therefore, instead of running from the discomfort or hiding from the fear in a bottle of booze, I can look within. There I can discover the cause of my imbalance and work toward growth and change. Then I can look around me, and even in the midst of chaos enjoy my own company.

Today: I will remember that ignoring or fleeing from the things that bother me will only allow them to fester. I will face my uneasiness today by praying to God for guidance and asking my support group for help.

DECEMBER 29

Give Something To Someone

It has been a good day if, when my head hits the pillow at night, I can answer yes to one of the following questions:

- Did I lighten the burden of another today?
- Did I listen intently while a friend spoke of hopes, worries, fears, joys, loves, trials, or triumphs?
- Did I do a favor for someone without them having to ask?
- Was I responsible to those who rely on me?
- Was I loving toward my family?
- Can I rest easy tonight, knowing that I served my fellow man throughout the day?

TODAY: I will remember to hold the door open for a stranger, call a friend I haven't seen in a while to say hello, or simply make lunch for my husband and put an "I love you" note in with it.

Only Addicts Can Truly Help Addicts

December 30

When I first accepted that there were certain substances over which I was powerless, I found it necessary to tell everyone in my life that I had the disease of addiction. I explained and explained and explained until I was blue in the face. I even gave them literature that would help them understand my illness. I thought if they learned more about the disease of addiction, they would be more helpful to me in my recovery.

Unfortunately, as much as my family and friends—who are not addicts—may want to help me, they can only do so much and learn so much, but never truly understand. Just as I have no idea what it is like to go through life as a blind person does, people who do not have an uncontrollable obsession with food, alcohol, gambling, or work cannot have any idea what that feels like. The only people who can really be of vital assistance are other recovering addicts.

Today: I will remember to look to those who have recovered from my addictions to assist me in my own recovery.

December 31

The Inner Light Of Hope

Although I wasn't always aware of it, hope has filled my inner being since before I was born. It has been the source of my strivings, my yearnings, and my dreams.

It has allowed me to try something different and it has opened my mind to ideas that may have once unnerved me. It has expanded my faith without me even knowing it. It is an unending reservoir from which I can take whenever I need. The only thing that blocks me from it is me.

When I am unwilling to grow, to learn, to trust—that is when I shut the door to the hope that lights me from within. And the only way to truly grow, to learn, and to trust, is to tap that inner light of hope.

Today: I will remember that hope is where I find the person I am meant to be today.

Index of Topics

About the Author

Jessica L. Morris lives in Pennsylvania with her husband and their cat, Lincoln. Along with a career of over twenty years in higher education advancement, for the past fifteen years she has been committed full-time to recovery from addictions and the relationship journey with her higher power. This second "career" has challenged all of her lifelong beliefs, for which she is forever grateful.

Jessica grew up with three siblings in small-town New Jersey, the daughter of an alcoholic minister. Her addiction to food is her earliest memory of childhood. Alcohol entered her life early, as well, and from there she endured a daily chase to find fulfillment in those two substances—which nearly resulted in death on several occasions. An obsession with boys and the need to be loved by everyone only added to the peril of her self-destructive path, but proved to be a blessing in disguise when a counselor suggested she seek recovery from her addictions.

Through the process of recovery and further counseling, Jessica began to feel an intense draw to understand and know God. Having been raised in such a confusing religious setting, she tread lightly at first. As part of her recovery, she began writing of the abuse she had suffered, the constant fear in which she lived, and the loneliness she experienced. She delved into her past, faced her own character limitations, and spoke honestly with the counselors who were trained to help her. As a result of these actions, she remained clean from the addictive substances that once ruled her life. She found internal peace and contentment that she never knew was possible.

Today, Jessica continues to search for a greater knowledge

of her higher power, who she knows is God. She has spent recent years devouring books about God, spirituality, and historical accounts of the life of Jesus and his last days on earth. She has turned to television shows and podcasts of ministers recommended by friends. And most recently, the call to continue learning God's word has compelled her to enroll in a seminary to work toward a master's degree.